Education, State and Crisis

Routledge Education Books

Advisory editor: John Eggleston
                     Professor of Education
                     University of Keele

Education, State and Crisis

A Marxist perspective

Madan Sarup

Goldsmiths' College
University of London

Routledge & Kegan Paul
London, Boston and Henley

First published in 1982
by Routlege & Kegan Paul Ltd
39 Store Street, London WC1E 7DD,
9 Park Street, Boston, Mass. 02108, USA and
Broadway House, Newtown Road,
Henley-on-Thames, Oxon RG9 1BN
Set in IBM Press Roman by
Columns, Reading
and printed in Great Britain by
T.J. Press Ltd, Padstow, Cornwall

Library of Congress Cataloging in Publication Data

Sarup, Madan.
Education, state and crisis.
(Routledge education books)
Includes bibliographical references and
index.
1. Education and state. 2. Educational
sociology. 3. Progressive education.
4. Marxian economics. I. Title. II. Series.
LC71.S24 370.19   81-17915

ISBN 0-7100-0956-9   AACR2
ISBN 0-7100-0959-3 (pbk.)

For John and James

Contents

Acknowledgments

Hardly a day passes without some news about what is happening in schools. Education is now a matter of public concern. This book, an outcome of teaching sociology at Goldsmiths' College, is an attempt to understand the redefinition that education is undergoing. Most of its themes have been discussed in lectures and seminars with colleagues and students and I would like to thank them for their support and stimulus. They have helped me to realize the many ways in which the institutions of the educational system are being restructured to achieve new goals. From them I have also learnt that 'education' has a metaphorical character, it has become a means for talking about many other things in society. In demonstrating this I am greatly indebted to many people whose ideas and books are fully acknowledged in the Notes. I am particularly grateful to David Yaffe for trying to teach me economics; John Colbeck, Pat Holland, Anne Kampendonk and Viv Parker criticized the text and suggested improvements. The help and encouragement of these, and many other friends, has been indispensable. I also wish to thank Penguin Books Ltd, Editions Gallimard and Random House Inc. for permission to quote from Michel Foucault, *Discipline and Punish*, 1977.

When you have thus formed the chain of ideas in the heads of your citizens, you will then be able to pride yourselves on guiding them and being their masters. A stupid despot may constrain his slaves with iron chains; but a true politician binds them even more strongly by the chain of their own ideas; it is at the stable point of reason that he secures the end of the chain; this link is all the stronger in that we do not know of what it is made and we believe it to be our own work; despair and time eat away the bonds of iron and steel, but they are powerless against the habitual union of ideas, they can only tighten it still more; and on the soft fibres of the brain is founded the unshakable base of the soundest of Empires.

J.Servan, 1780, quoted by Michel Foucault,
Discipline and Punish, p. 102.

Preface

Many exciting developments are taking place in the 'sociology of education'. It is being transformed, revitalized, by the contributions of history, economics, Marxism, feminism, and black studies. The social and political climate is also changing rapidly as our work in schools, our lives, are being affected by a phenomenon new to most of us: the economic crisis. Gradually it is being realized that the numerous, seemingly disparate changes taking place in education are but a manifestation of this deeper crisis which is a world-wide crisis of capitalism.

This short text is a critical survey of current educational debates. It focuses on the themes which have taken on a new urgency and importance: the problematic nature of 'progressive' education and 'discipline', the changes in the labour process and youth unemployment; the nature of the state and its relationship with schooling; the growth of state intervention; the specific forms of discrimination that women and black people suffer in schools and in a society undergoing an economic crisis.

It is argued that to understand these processes fully the study of some economics is necessary. I think that one of the most serious shortcomings of education courses in this country is their complete neglect of economics. Students are not being given the opportunities to gain the knowledge that will enable them to understand the structural changes that are taking place in their world. One of the aims of this book, therefore, is to link the discussion of recent developments in sociological theory and education with some basic Marxist economics. It will be argued that we are witnessing an attack on progessivism; an increasing emphasis on discipline at a time of unemployment; an increase of ideological pressures in schools and the growth of state intervention. What is the relationship between these tendencies and how are they to be explained? Let us begin our analysis of recent controversies by examining some of the attacks on progressive education.

Chapter 1

The attack on progressive education

Introduction

As the economic and social crisis develops more and more people are asking: What are schools for? Has progressivism failed? What should be the relationship between schools and industry? Why is there increasing state intervention in education? These themes have been taken up by capitalist organizations and trade unions, by parents and politicians, by teachers and students. The media, too, have been quick to take up the new interest in the politics of education.

Let me begin the story in 1976; in that year Prime Minister James Callaghan gave a speech in which he criticized education for failing to provide pupils with the basic skills necessary for industry. The schools, he said, were failing to prepare children for their role in the economy. The Minister of Education endorsed this view and regional conferences were arranged. The topics discussed are significant: the school curriculum, the assessment of standards, teacher training, schools and working life.

It is now apparent that it was decided by the Department of Education and Science (DES), before the 'Great Debate', that there had to be more effective control of the content of the school curriculum: the DES increased its control of the Schools Council, an institution largely concerned with the creation of new curricular approaches. There was talk of a 'common core' curriculum, and the DES set up the Assessment of Performance Unit whose task is to formulate methods of national monitoring of standards of achievement in maths, language and science teaching in schools.

In the 'Debate' there was no discussion of the DES itself and its role. Nor was there any discussion of the financing of education and the question of available economic resources. But how did the debate come about and why was it instituted? It would be inadequate to analyse

1

these events only in terms of 'pressure groups'. The concept of a large number of shifting pressure groups coalescing over different issues, is a liberal view of power. A historical materialist analysis would see these 'groups' as representing fundamental economic interests, and the events as expressions of class struggle. One hypothesis is that the Right was becoming vociferous in its criticisms of education; it was being said that moral and educational standards were falling drastically and that the Labour Party tried in a defensive reaction to capture the initiative from the conservative Right. It could also be said that the debate about education was a ploy, a distraction from increasing unemployment and factory closures. At a time of economic crisis, the educational debate was an attempt to shift the responsibility for the crisis on to the schools when the causes lay elsewhere.

But the crisis is not only an economic crisis, it is also political and ideological; though its source may be economic, there are expressions of the crisis in education. Consider the development of the following events: In the dispute at William Tyndale School, London, the teachers were accused of left-wing political indoctrination. Many of the teachers used progressive methods and so child-centred education was blamed for declining standards. A year later, in 1976, Neville Bennett's book *Teaching Styles and Pupils' Progress* was published; it suggested that children taught by informal methods made less 'progress' than those taught by formal methods. These 'moral panics' were not isolated happenings; they were a developing sequence of events orchestrated by the press.[1] Suddenly, teaching became too important to be left to teachers. The old consensus was broken and there was a call for new controls. External agencies, such as the Assessment of Performance Unit, were therefore set up to monitor standards and control teachers' work. The Gould Report followed in 1977, asserting that 'Marxists' should be excluded from educational institutions. There was the re-emergence of genetic theories, like those of Jenson and Eysenck, utilized by fascist groups, which made racism in education a vital issue. These disparate empirical events are connected; they illustrate a fundamental shift in the structure of the British social formation and its institutions. What are the main characteristics of this shift in the field of education? They are: the attack on progressivism, the enforcement of stricter discipline, the emphasis on work-socialization, and the increasing concentration of power. These problems, which have to be analysed and explained, are the central themes of the following chapters. Let us now begin with a consideration of progressivism; after noting (schematically) some of the differing stances towards it, we will examine two critiques of progressivism, the first one stemming from the Left, and the second one from the Right.

The disagreement about progressivism

Progressivism, which was popularized in the 1960s at the height of the economic 'boom', can be said to be the mode of education where the child, considered to be the centre of the educational process, largely chooses activities according to its own needs and interests. In such a mode there is a rejection of imposed discipline and external authority, of the excessive use of punishment on the one hand, and extrinsic rewards on the other. A movement against inert, meaningless learning, it attempts to dissolve the distinction between 'work' and 'play'. But such definitions do not really help us; the problem is: what functions does it perform? What does it really do? There seems to be no agreement, as the following attitudes towards progressivism show:

1 some believe that progressivism is a form of romanticism, a spontaneous ideology which has an anti-intellectualist stress on self-fulfilment; they are therefore critical of it. For example, Brian Simon, a leading communist educationalist, is fiercely critical of progressivism because it 'explicitly denies the need for systematization and structure. The roots of progressivism lie in anarcho-liberalism. Such ideas . . . lead to a kind of romantic revolutionism that denies the need for political action and sees the isolated classroom as the focus and lever for social change.'[2]

2 There are others, like Samuel Bowles and Herbert Gintis, who think that progressivism is a good idea but has never been practised. They write: 'thus there are some grounds for the opinion that the modern liberal view of the self-developmental capacities of schooling has not been falsified by recent U.S. experience; rather it has never been tried.'[3]

3 Some argue that progressivism is genuinely 'progressive' in the sense that it is inimical to capitalist discipline. Progressivism has provided space for left-wing teachers, and that is the reason for recent attacks upon it by the political Right.

4 Against the above view, other theorists argue that progressivism is merely a more subtle, sophisticated method of socialization under the guise of an apparent freedom. Progressivism and the innovations associated with it give participants the impression that authoritarianism is not present, but usually this is not the case. A characteristic of bourgeois education in general is that it presents mental production as an act of the isolated individual mind. Solutions to most problems are seen in terms of individual psychology; individualist theories are the basis of progressivism. Subjectivist individualism and phenomenological approaches, it is argued, should be regarded sceptically at a time when collective, social, structural changes are urgently required. This view is most clearly expressed in the study to which we now turn.

The attack on progressivism from the Left

At the time Sharp and Green were writing *Education and Social Control*, which is a study of progressive primary education, the social-phenomenological research was very influential. This approach, used by the 'New Sociology of Education', was individualistic; it stressed consciousness and ignored power structures and economic determinants. In contrast, Sharp and Green wanted to develop a *materialist* viewpoint.[4] They challenged the ideology of child-centredness - the notion that there are ethical, psychological, sociological and pedagogical reasons for considering the individual child as the teachers' central concern.

The authors studied three infant classes, the teachers and the parents in a progressive school in a homogeneous working-class area. What did the researchers find? The children, given a wide discretion to choose between many activities, had to satisfy their teachers that they were 'busy'. It seemed that the teachers were rather unclear about their own precise role and how they were going to further their pupils' knowledge. The rationale of the teachers had strong undertones of two perspectives: 'deprivation' and 'social pathology'. These theories stress that working-class children and those of ethnic minorities are culturally deprived and/or genetically deficient. The school functioned as a socializing institution to 'civilize' the deprived; in this way the teachers legitimized their therapeutic ideology.

Whilst the teachers displayed a moral concern that every child mattered, in practice there was a subtle process of sponsorship developing where opportunity was being offered to some and closed off to others. Moreover, there was not merely a developing hierarchy of pupils, but the content of education was being selectively organized and transmitted. In the authors' view, 'the social structuring of the pupils' identities can be seen as the intial stages of the institutionalization of social selection for the stratification system.' Education in this view, then, is a crucial mechanism for socialization and social control, initiating people into those skills, attitudes, and values which are essential for effective role performance. It is thus involved in social selection and role allocation.[5]

Their argument is that educational institutions have 'a crucial role to play in the reproduction of socio-economic systems that depend at one level on the production of human capital through the inculcation of knowledge and skill and at another level on the social transmission of varying levels of ignorance'.[6] In other words, industrial societies are faced with the problem both of satisfying a demand for skilled and trained personnel, and of providing some institutional means for soaking up or consuming surplus labour which results from advancing technology.

Thus Sharp and Green believe that the character of interaction, and the perspectives of the actors involved, may camouflage the real structure of relationships in which groups and individuals are embedded:[7] whilst educators and parents may view the educational system as the locale where talent is developed and individual needs responded to, its 'real' function may be very different and related more to the social demands of established interests in the macro structure than to the requirements of individual pupils.

These authors argue that the rise of progressivism and the institutional support that it receives are a function of its *greater effectiveness for social control and structuring aspirations* compared with more traditional educational ideologies whose legitimacy was already being questioned. Within child-centred progressivism, far wider ranges of the child's attributes become legitimate objects of evaluative scrutiny.[8]

In short, the researchers found that teachers often used a rhetoric to hide certain features; they found explanations which hide the fact that classrooms reproduced hierarchies or that certain children's identities were being reified (that is, treated as natural rather than social products) through labelling. Though teachers often said that children should develop their own needs and interests, underlying this was an unexplicated assumption that children should develop their needs and interests 'according to the community'. The term 'guided discovery', for example, was used with a different stress at different times for the purpose of self-justification. Indeed, teachers thought of themselves as experts, and this separated them from parents, who were cast in a passive role.

According to Sharp and Green, the educational ideology of child-centred progressivism fails to comprehend the realities of a stratified society where facilities, prestige and rewards are unequally distributed. It cannot explain these phenomena but takes them as given. The authors believe that a progressive educator, whose Utopian solutions are ineffective, is little more than an unwilling apologist for the system. Modern child-centred education is an aspect of romantic, radical conservatism. It involves an emotional turning away from society, an attempt to bring about a change of individual consciousness. This romantic conservatism is very influential, and it underlies not only progressivism in the state primary sector but also the deschooling movement.

Education and Social Control, then, presents an argument against the liberal individualism of progressive educators; it is an attack on child-centred education and the so-called radicals who support it. The research draws our attention to one of the dilemmas of progressive education: whilst it stressed the development of autonomy and the self, it inevitably provides a socializing environment — but one in which the

5

rules and principles are not made explicit. On the other hand, it could be argued that in truly progressive education the rules of socialization could become explicit. But it should be noted that Sharp and Green's attack is directed against progressive education in state schools. In my view, most of these schools have either never really practised it, or practiced only 'watered down' versions of the principles proposed by pioneers such as A.S. Neill.

My main criticism of the study is that Sharp and Green do not have have a theory of the relationship between the economic base and the superstructure. (By 'base' I am referring to the forces and relations of production; by the term 'superstructure' I mean both the level of political and legal institutions, and the level of ideology, culture, theory and consciousness.) This is partly a question of the relationship between the 'micro' and 'macro' levels of society. The authors state that Marxist work on the interrelationship between childhood and education is underdeveloped.[9] There is a lack of adequate concepts and theory for the study of ideological aspects of interaction in schools. It may be noticed that though the book is a critique of idealism the methodology used is that of symbolic interactionism (a notoriously un-materialist approach which stresses that human beings are active agents in the construction and interpretation of social situations and their meanings). Sharp and Green, lacking a consistent approach and vocabulary, tend to be eclectic.

Moreover, they do not address the question of the place of the teacher in the class structure. Is the teacher a productive or unproductive worker? This is an important question for me because through it I have begun to see how the educational sector is related to the productive forces and the relations of production. I will develop this point in a later chapter.

Nevertheless, Sharp and Green do raise important issues: is progressivism or 'libertarianism' a more subtle form of social control — a cloak for manipulation? Perhaps some teachers used progressivism because it does enable them to do something practical — at least seating arrangements can be changed even though the struggle to change structures is a harder task. Is progressivism, then, merely a 'managerial solution', or has it provided a space for left-wing teachers to develop elements of a Marxist pedagogy? That there are opposing views can be clearly demonstrated by considering the attack on progressivism not only from the Left but from the Right.

The attack on progressivism from the Right

As representative of the many attacks on progressivism from the Right, let us consider Neville Bennett's research on *Teaching Styles and*

Pupils' Progress.[10] He asks: What is the relationship between teaching style and pupil attainment? Believing that there may be a waste of money and human potential in some present teaching styles, he asks: are children learning enough? In his view many of the assumptions of the Plowden Report (1967) have remained untested; though the Report is committed to progressivism, he could find no research evidence for it. Let me, first, outline his research before describing the importance that it gained in the political climate of the time.

Bennett began his research by sending out questionnaires to 871 primary schools in Cumbria and Lancashire. There was an 88% response, and a 'cluster' analysis produced twelve teaching styles. Three dozen classes and thirty-seven teachers who taught in three general teaching styles, (informal, mixed, and formal) were closely scrutinized. According to Bennett's categories, the informal school stressed the notion of self-motivation, and the formal school believed in giving children security. In the formal school the teacher taught the children by telling them directly, and work was clearly separated from play. The research found that achievement in reading, arithmetic, and English was better in the formal school. Only the less able did relatively well in the informal school, but the research programme ignored these children. Bennett, who was himself educated in a progressive school, has stated that what interests him is the problem: what aspects of formal teaching can be useful to the progressive teacher? He contends that the informal style of teaching is only successful where there is sequencing of the curriculum; that is to say, where the teacher has *structured* the content for the pupils.

Now, unlike Sharp and Green, whose work is Marxist, Bennett claims to be 'value-free'. I will not recapitulate here the numerous methodological criticisms that have been made — his research has all the shortcomings of positivist methodology. Though he believes he can evaluate accurately because, after all, teachers evaluate their teaching every day, Bennett's form of evaluation is always based on statistical measurement, and this, of course, means that only the measurable is measured, and that which is not easily measurable is not regarded as significant.

What is important about Bennett's book is not what is contained within it, but how it came to be *used* in the ideological struggle. The book was commented on by the whole range of the press who treated it as if it was a government publication: 'the Bennett Report'. It was made news. The press exploited the research by linking formal teaching with standards, discipline and order; informal teaching with no discipline, chaos. Thus the press contributed to a hardening of the definition of the terms of the debate. Progressive teaching was associated with falling standards and left-wing teachers; formal teaching with the upholding of standards, the interests of parents, and 'good sense'.

Whilst the media manipulated concern about standards in schools, there was a barrage of criticism from employers against a school system which produced young people who lacked basic skills, who would not accept orders enthusiastically, or did not get up in the morning to go to work at the assembly line. Gradually, all sorts of pressures increased on teachers to emphasize reading and numeracy; rote-learning and testing became even more common.

Having given an exposition of two critiques of progressivism, from the Left and the Right, I now want to make a qualification: it is not always possible to make neat, clear-cut categorizations about what is, and what is not, 'progressive'. For example, the aims and practices of institutions may change gradually and they may develop contradictory features.

An example, not perhaps strictly related to progressivism but, nevertheless, concerned with 'openness and control', is an interesting critique of the Open University.[11] It illustrates the process of how some institutions, when set up, are envisaged as having progressive aims, but may gradually develop features contrary to their original goals. Dave Harris and John Holmes have written about how the Open University represented for many people a 'second chance', an opening up of education, the realization of a Fabian ideal. But what has happened to this large, highly admired institution? First, the ideal of 'openness' has given way to impersonality and indifference. The past and present interests of the students are largely ignored by a highly centralized bureaucracy. Second, the stress on clear exposition has led to a constraint on presentations, and a 'tight' teaching system. Third, assessment which was originally meant to be diagnostic, has become a fixed distribution of grades. Fourth, most of the courses have come to be seen as facts to be regurgitated. As learning is individualized, most students have no opportunity for constructing alternative meanings and viewpoints.

The writers, Harris and Holmes, have related what Ralph Turner called 'contest' and 'sponsored mobility' to the Open University (contest mobility is like an open sporting event in which many compete for a few prizes; sponsored mobility is rather like induction into a club, the recruits being chosen by the established elite).[12] They argue that the Open University appears to work in a mode which has features characteristic of 'contest mobility'. There is continuous testing and a high drop-out rate, and so the student, painfully isolated, requires a high level of ambition. Now, though the Open University appears to further contest mobility, in reality it is a new form of sponsored mobility. Moreover, the emphasis at the Open University is on cost-effectiveness and its staff have become packagers of knowledge.[13] Thus, what was once established as a progressive institution and could be seen as liberating, is now a form of 'education' suitable, in its methods, for a fascist state.

Individualism and the failure of social reform

Before discussing some of the difficulties of the concept, let me put progressive education in a wider historical and political context and relate it to the developments in the sociology of education. The assumption that the individual is more important than the group or class was held by many politicians, educationalists and social reformers who, after the Second World War, institutionalized a common examination (the '11 plus'). Children were then sent to grammar, technical or secondary modern schools. This tripartite system, which emerged after the 1944 Act, was supposed to provide a genuine equality of opportunity, a more meritocratic distribution of opportunities and rewards. But what happened? The better-off mobilized the resources of the free education system to the benefit of their children. And so, in fact, a working-class boy's chance of obtaining a selective education changed little between the 1920s and the 1950s. Indeed, the likelihood of a working-class boy getting a grammar-school education in the mid-1950s was very little different from that of his parents' generation seventy years earlier. Thus, a class-based system, with the public schools at the top and the secondary modern schools at the bottom, survived the social upheaval of the post-war years largely intact.[14]

Not surprisingly, there was a shift in focus; there followed debates about cultural deprivation, 'disadvantage'; then came the institutionalization of 'enrichment programmes', the setting up of 'Educational Priority Areas' to compensate for the 'deficits' of working-class people.

Several other approaches in the sociology of education overlapped with the one outlined above; I will briefly mention three of them. They focused, broadly, on the organization of the school, the teacher-pupil interaction, and the curriculum. Some researchers, focusing on the internal organization of the school, draw attention to the effects of streaming. It was argued, for example, that the streaming system actually contributed to bringing about what it was supposed to solve.[15] Besides the formal organization, other aspects of the school were analysed; some researchers specialized on teacher-pupil interaction.[16] This included considerable work on language which centred on the question: in what ways does language contribute to working-class failure? What is it that teachers 'hear', or rather 'don't hear' when listening to working-class pupils?

The 'new sociology of education', initially inspired by phenomenology (particularly the work of Michael F.D. Young, Nell Keddie, and Geoff Esland), focused on the curriculum. These radical sociologists, reacting against the determinism of Parsonian functionalism, adopted symbolic interactionism (Mead, Geoffman) and social phenomenology (Schutz, Cicourel, Garfinkel) as alternative conceptions of society and doing sociology. At the same time, many radical teachers, antagonistic to the 'banking' notion of education, in which pupils are thought of as passive receptacles, embraced progressivism. Neither the progressive teachers nor the new sociologists of education fully realized the individualist, liberal, subjectivist assumptions underlying their beliefs.[17]

I have suggested in the above section that a characteristic feature shared by government policies and these theoretical perspectives was a belief in individualism. Indeed, I would contend that there are some similarities between progressivism in schools and the phenomenological approach of the 'new sociology of education'. Both stress the wishes, the expectations and the rationality of the individual agent. Both give pupils a (false) sense of freedom.[18] Moreover, there is an extreme, voluntaristic stress on consciousness that denies the existence of real power exercised by the dominating class.

It has already been remarked that the progressive approach has often been considered in an over-simplified way, as if it was some easily identifiable, unproblematic brand of education. The roots of progressivism spring from so many diverse sources, from the liberal pragmatism of John Dewey to the Utopian socialism/anarchism of Paul Goodman, that different 'progressive' teachers could, in practice, educate children in different ways, following incompatible policies. So much seems to depend on who (practitioners, critics, the media) calls what practice 'progressive'. But, in spite of the ambiguities, there is something distinctive about the progressive approach; it asserts that activities should not be imposed from above, but that pupils should be encouraged to develop themselves. The stress is on learning from 'where the pupil is' in terms of his or her interests, and on the relevance of knowledge; in this sense it is child-centred rather than subject-centred.

I want to suggest that progressivism can be theorized on three levels: (1) the Rhetoric of progressivism is that which is merely talked about. (2) The Practice of progressivism: this is the descriptive level which refers to what actually goes on in schools. (3) The Ideal: the prescriptive level which refers to what should be the case, what ought to go on in schools.

Such a conceptualization helps to explain why both the Left and the Right attack progressivism. When the Left attack, they are focusing their criticisms on the rhetoric of progressivism and its (non)practice. When the Right attack progressivism, they are doing it at the prescriptive level which they see as influencing actual practice in schools. I have to admit, however, that progressive education is not practised extensively in schools. Where it is genuinely practised (and not 'watered down'), it is potentially inimical to capitalist discipline – this is one of the reasons why progressivism is attacked by the Right.

Nevertheless, there are some cogent arguments against some forms of progressive education *from the Left* which should be seriously considered. First, though progressive education stresses the needs and interests of children, it ignores the fact that when pupils come to school they are not all capable of exploiting the resources offered by the school. The uneven distribution of what Bourdieu has called 'cultural capital' is ignored.[19]

Second, child-centred education takes insufficient account of the fact that capitalism actually limits the extent to which children's inner potential or consciousness may be allowed to develop. This is because the main functions of schooling are to discipline the future workforce, to grade it, to provide certain limited skills and to 'child-mind' it. When the economy expands, 'concessions' are made to progressivism, but in periods of crisis these functions of the state educational system become clearer to see. Schools act as custodians and reproduce the social relations of capitalism.

Third, it could be said that progressivism is an alternative to the dominant practice – but it is not oppositional. Raymond Williams has made the useful distinction between *alternative* and *oppositional*, that is to say,[20]

> between someone who simply finds a different way to live and
> wishes to be left alone with it, and someone who finds a different
> way to live and wants to change society in its light. This is usually
> the distinction between individual and small-group solutions to
> social crisis and those solutions which properly belong to political
> and ultimately revolutionary practice.

The concept of political practice and ideological struggle is related to another argument; progressivism originally may have had radical objectives, but it has often been taken up for purposes of control. Paul Willis has described how some ground is yielded to pupils and their points of view in the interest of ensuring a more basic control.[21] (How this control and definition is supported and underwritten in countless ways, such as the architecture, the organization and the practices of the school will be shown in the next chapter.) This tactical withdrawal for strategic containment is legitimated with the rhetoric of progressivism. The justification is often in terms of 'individual learning', 'discovery', 'self-direction', and 'relevance'. 'Progressivism' is sometimes even used for the justification and rationalization of existing tendencies when traditional models are failing or being threatened. In other words, an outright confrontation is often avoided through the use of 'liberal' methods, but again these concessions and tactical withdrawals are only made to ensure firmer control.

Willis also conceptualizes progressivism on three levels which he terms the official, the pragmatic, and the cultural. He argues that at the official level, 'progressivism' has been developed as an acceptable ideology by academics in conjunction with wider social democratic movements to increase educational opportunities for the working class. At the pragmatic level, progressivism has sometimes been taken up in schools as a practical solution to practical problems without any real shift in basic philosophies of education. Third, at the cultural level, it could be argued that often 'progressivism' has had the contradictory and unintended effect of helping to strengthen processes within schools which are responsible for the subordination of the working class, processes which are the very opposite of progressive intentions in education.[22]

Given that thirty years of highly financed research and a considerable amount of time and effort have been expended, why does the problem of working-class 'failure' still exist? I suggest that one valid response is to argue that in the traditional approaches the study of pupils, knowledge and schools is separated from the structual aspects, such as the forces and relations of production which arise from *the mode of production*. We need to study the location and exercise of power. Who has power and how is it utilized? How is class power legitimated?

Let us return for a moment to the issue with which we began: consciousness of self, the role of the individual. We are continually being told that in our 'free' (competitive) society the individual can be a success through hard work and self-help. But the notion that human beings are (or should be) separate entities, each metaphorically surrounded by an inviolable area of individuality within which reside our 'individual' rights, our 'individual' psyche, our 'individual' personality, is fairly recent, a relatively modern development connected with the rise of (protestantism and) capitalism. Because the concept of individualism is used for ideological purposes, it is often not fully realized that there is a difference between the logic of an individual's interests and the logic of class interest. As Paul Willis has pointed out:[23]

> To the *individual* working-class person mobility in this society may mean something. Some working-class individuals do 'make it' and any particular individual may hope to be one of them. To the class or group at its own proper level however, mobility, means nothing at all. The only true mobility at this level would be the destruction of the whole class society.

In other words, the school stresses hard work, diligence, conformism, factual knowledge as the prescriptions for success. These are the false individualistic premises of dominant ideology as they operate in the school. Conformism may hold a certain logic for the individual, but for the class it holds no rewards. The school generalizes from the individualistic logic to a group logic; the contradiction is never admitted that not all can succeed. In short, a few can 'make it'; the class can never follow. It is through a good number of individuals trying, however, that the class structure is legitimated.

In this chapter I have attempted to explore the problematic nature of 'progressivism' and have argued that it is not possible to make neat, clear-cut categorizations because there are differing views about the rhetoric, the practice and the ideal of progressivism. These 'levels' are always changing their character and institutions may develop contradictory features. The problems that I have described are not new ones; as education is a field of political and ideological struggle there is a constant process of incorporation, then retrieval, radical innovatory advance, followed again by incorporation and containment. Whether teachers should be committed to (certain forms of) progressivism or be against it may well depend on the particular circumstances of the time. I mentioned some of the numerous attacks by the Right on aspects of progressivism and have tried to provide some of the reasons why Left groups were unable to co-ordinate their strategy. This failure provided space for a new backlash from the Right. Now, as the crisis develops, there is an increasing emphasis on 'law and order' in society. This is mirrored in the schools, where there is a shift from progressivism to more direct styles of instruction associated with the re-assertion of authority and discipline.

Chapter 2

The enforcement of discipline

Introduction

The assault on progressive education can be seen as one feature of the trend towards the enforcement of stricter discipline. In the last chapter it was suggested that some aspects of progressivism, in certain circumstances, can be used as a subtle means of greater social control. This can be illustrated by the ideology of 'pastoral care'.

Pastoral care in schools is based on a 'personal' knowledge of pupils and help is given to deal with their problems. But, at some stage, other agencies are called in. What may appear as a compassionate concern for the individual child is really an attempt to socialize the 'deviant'. Pastoral care thus becomes an inculcation of the 'expressive order'. It is often said that teachers are working for the children's 'best interests', but usually pastoral care directly supports the structure, discipline and values of the school. There is now a move towards having a welfare officer based at the school. Lateness and attendance patterns are investigated by educational psychologists, as they may reveal an underlying 'problem'. Other social services are bought in. There are tutorial classes at home, sanctuaries, 'sin-bins', remedial centres. With the increasing intervention of the state, there is a growth in the ideology of pastoral care, involving teachers, social workers, police and doctors in this problem, the problem of youth 'discipline' and 'order'.

I want to argue that these features are now commonplace, they are characteristic of all schools. Pupils are observed and their conduct is noted daily. They are divided up not only according to their abilities, but also according to the dispositions that they reveal. The school has become a sort of permanent observatory where the pupil is subjected to habits, rules, orders, examinations. The obedient subject is constructed by a technique: discipline.

But how did this process begin? An important account has been provided by Michel Foucault who, in *Discipline and Punish*, has examined the origin and development of these processes in society.[1] What interests Foucault is the process by which, in eighty years (1760-1840), penal detention replaced public execution as a calculated technique for altering individual behaviour. He notes how torture during public executions, punishment as spectacle, was replaced by the penalties of prison. The right to punish shifted from the vengeance of the sovereign to 'the defence of society'. Foucault writes in vivid detail of the shift in the eighteenth century to stricter methods of surveillance, a tighter partitioning of the population, more efficient techniques of locating and obtaining information. He describes how under cover of the relative stability of the law, a mass of subtle and rapid changes occurred: a gradual extension of the mechanisms of *discipline*. There is a growth of the ways of defining an individual under the pretext of explaining an action. Judgment is passed, not only on crimes and offences, but also on passions, instincts, drives and desires, infirmities, maladjustments. What is considered is not only what people do, but also what they are, will be, may be. To decide whether an act was produced by environment or heredity, the instincts, or the unconscious, requires a whole set of assessing, diagnostic, prognostic, normative judgments. It was in the eighteenth century, then, that as a result of new constraints and strict rules, a whole army of technicians gradually took over from the executioner: the wardens, doctors, chaplains, psychiatrists, psychologists, educationalists. I shall now focus on those aspects of Foucault's book that relate specifically to the school.

The school as a disciplinary and grading mechanism

The organization of space and time

The classical age discovered the body as object and target of power; it became aware that the body can be used, manipulated, shaped, trained, made to obey. Many of the disciplinary methods had long been in existence, in monasteries, armies, and workshops, but in the course of the seventeenth and eighteenth centuries the '*disciplines*', the insights and techniques of the human sciences, became general formulae of domination. What was new was that by being combined and generalized they attained a level at which the formation of knowledge and the increase of power regularly reinforced one another in a circular process.

In the first instance, discipline proceeds from the distribution of individuals in space; discipline requires enclosure. And so we see the gradual imposition of the monastic model in secondary schools where

15

boarding became the most frequent regime. That there is a need to distribute and partition off space in a rigorous manner can be seen in the development of factories. Production was divided up and each variable of the workforce — strength, promptness, skill — was observed, assessed, computed. The organization of *serial* space was also important: by assigning individual places it made possible the supervision of each individual and the simultaneous work of all. It made the educational space function like a learning-machine, but also as a machine for supervising, hierarchizing, rewarding. It organized a new economy of time.

An important part is played by the timetable. Originating in the monasteries, where for centuries the religious orders had been specialists in the use of rhythm and regular activities, this technique soon spread and was to be found in schools, workshops, and hospitals. In the elementary schools the division of time became increasingly minute, and activities were governed in detail by orders that had to be obeyed immediately. In the early nineteenth century the following timetable was suggested for the French 'mutual improvement schools': 8.45 entrance of the monitor, 8.52 the monitor's summons, 8.56 entrance of the children and prayer, 9.00 the children go to their benches, 9.04 first slate, 9.08 end of dictation, 9.12 second slate, etc.[2]

An attempt was made to assure the quality of the time used through constant supervision, the pressure of supervisors, the elimination of anything that might disturb or distract. Nothing must remain idle or useless. It was a question of constituting a totally useful time. Precision and application are, with regularity, the fundamental virtues of disciplinary time.

Now, the activities of disciplined individuals require a precise system of command. Orders have to be brief and clear; what is important is perceiving the signal and reacting to it immediately. Thus, the training of school-children was carried out in total silence, interrupted only by signals. Indeed, in the eighteenth century there was a wooden apparatus called the 'Signal':[3]

> When the prayer has been said the teacher will strike the signal at once and, turning to the child whom he wishes to read, he will make the sign to begin. To make a sign to stop to a pupil who is reading, he will strike the signal once . . . To make a sign to a pupil to repeat when he had read badly . . . he will strike the signal twice in rapid succession. If, after the sign has been made two or three times, the pupil who is reading does not find and repeat the word that he has badly read or mispronounced . . . the teacher will strike three times in rapid succession, as a sign to him to begin to read farther back.

The imposition of disciplinary time had the following effects:

specializing the time of training and detaching it from adult time; arranging different stages, separated from one another by graded examinations; drawing up programmes, each of which had to take place during a particular stage and which involved exercises of increasing difficulty; qualifying individuals according to the way in which they progress through these series. Foucault describes the organization of a school of drawing in 1737 for tapestry apprentices:[4]

> The pupils performed individual tasks at regular intervals; each of these exercises, signed with the name of its author and date of execution, was handed in to the teacher; the best were rewarded; assembled together at the end of the year and compared, they made it possible to establish the progress, the present ability and the relative place of each pupil; it was then decided which of them could pass into the next class. A general book kept by the teachers and their assistants, recorded from day to day the behaviour of the pupils and everything that happened in the school; it was periodically shown to an inspector.

In the eighteenth century a whole analytical pedagogy was formed, meticulous in its detail. It broke down the subject taught into its simplest elements, it hierarchized each stage of development into small steps. This made possible a detailed control and regular intervention. In this process, *exercise* is vital — the technique by which one imposes on the body tasks that are both repetitive and different, but always graduated. The idea of an educational programme that would follow the child to the end of his schooling and which would involve from year to year, month to month, exercises of increasing complexity was of religious origin. Discipline, then, operates the following techniques: it draws up tables, it prescribes movements, it imposes a permanent competition of individuals in relation to one another. But what is the chief function of disciplinary power?

The role of examinations

Discipline trains individuals; it 'makes' them. It is a specific technique of power that regards individuals both as objects and instruments of its exercise. The exercise of discipline presupposes a mechanism that coerces by means of *observation*. For a long time the model of the military camp (where power is exercised through observation of eyes that see without being seen) was found in urban development, in the construction of working-class housing estates, hospitals, prisons — and schools. The old architecture was for confinement and enclosure, thick walls, heavy gates that prevented entering or leaving; this began to be replaced in the seventeenth and eighteenth centuries by buildings where it was possible for a single gaze to see everything constantly: the new architecture was to 'permit an internal, articulated, and detailed control – to render visible those who are inside it; in more general terms, an architecture that would operate to transform individuals: to act on those it shelters, to provide a hold on their conduct, to carry the effects of power right to them, to make it possible to know them, to alter them.'[5]

Thus hierarchized, continuous and functional surveillance was insidiously extended; 'the workshop, the school, the army were subject to a whole micro-penalty of time (latenesses, absences, interruptions of tasks), of activity (inattention, negligence, lack of zeal), of behaviour (impoliteness, disobedience), of speech (idle chatter, insolence), of the body ('incorrect' attitudes, irregular features, lack of cleanliness), of sexuality (impurity, indecency).'[6] It is through the 'disciplines' that the power of the Norm appears. The Normal is established as a principle of coercion. In teaching, it appears with the introduction of a standardized education and the teachers' training colleges. Like surveillance, and with it, *normalization* became one of the great instruments of power.

The institution that combines the techniques of an observing hierarchy and those of a normalizing judgment is the *examination*. Examinations, disciplinary writing, made it possible to form categories to determine averages, to fix norms. The school has become increasingly concerned with the perpetual comparison of pupils. The purpose of examinations is to rank. Foucault writes:[7]

> rows or ranks of pupils in the class, corridors, court yards; rank attributed to each pupil at the end of each task and each examination, the rank he obtains from week to week, month to month, year to year; an alignment of age groups, one after another; a succession of subjects taught and questions treated, according to an order of increasing difficulty. And in this ensemble of compulsory alignments, each pupil, according to his age, his performance, his behaviour, occupies sometimes one rank, sometimes another, he moves constantly over a series of compartments – some of these are 'ideal' compartments, making a hierarchy of knowledge or ability, others express the distribution of values or merits in material terms in the space of the college or classroom. It is a perpetual movement in which individuals replace one another in a space marked off by aligned intervals.

Examinations make each 'individual' a case. Foucault suggests that the child, the patient, the madman and the prisoner become the objects of individual descriptions and biographical accounts. By the continuous calculation of plus and minus points the disciplinary apparatuses hierarchize the 'good' and the 'bad' in relation to one another. (We shall be discussing these processes further in the last part of this chapter.) This distribution according to ranks or grades has a double role: it marks the gaps, hierarchizes qualities, skills and aptitudes, but it also punishes and rewards. For Foucault, 'the examination as the fixing, at once ritual and "scientific", of individual differences, as the pinning down of each individual ... clearly indicates the appearance of a new modality of power.'[8]

Examinations nowadays appear in the form of tests, interrogations, interviews, and consultations — apparently in order to rectify the mechanisms of discipline. Just as the medical or psychiatric interview is supposed to rectify the effects of the discipline of work, educational psychology is supposed to correct the rigours of the school. Actually, these techniques merely refer individuals from one disciplinary authority to another.

Panopticism

One of Foucault's key concepts is panopticism. This is how he describes Jeremy Bentham's architectural design, the Panopticon:[9]

> At the periphery, an annular building; at the centre, a tower; this tower is pierced with wide windows that open onto the inner side of the ring; the peripheric building is divided into cells, each of which extends the whole width of the building; they have two windows, one on the inside, corresponding to the windows of the tower; the other, on the outside, allows the light to cross the cell from one end to the other. All that is needed, then, is to place a supervisor in a central tower and to shut up in each cell a madman, a patient, a condemned man, a worker, or a schoolboy. By the effect of backlighting, one can observe from the tower, standing out precisely against the light, the small captive shadows in the cells of the periphery. They are like so many cages, so many small theatres, in which each actor is alone, perfectly individualized and constantly visible.

Each individual is seen but does not see; he is the object of information, never a subject in communication.

The Panopticon arranges things so that surveillance is permanent, even if it is discontinuous in its action. The inmate is aware that s/he may be observed at any one moment. This architectural apparatus, then, is a machine for creating and sustaining a power relation independent of the person who exercises it. The perfection of this power

19

should tend to render its actual exercise unnecessary; the inmates are caught up in a power situation of which they are themselves the bearers. In view of this, Bentham laid down the principle that power should be visible and unverifiable. In the peripheric ring, one is totally seen without ever seeing; in the central tower, one sees everything without ever being seen. And so it is not necessary to use force to constrain the convict to good, the madman to calm, the worker to work, the schoolboy to application.

If there are children in the spaces, there is no copying, no talking, no waste of time; they are a collection of separated individualities that can be numbered and supervised. It is possible to observe performances, to map aptitudes, to assess characters, to draw up rigorous classifications. But the Panopticon is also a laboratory, a machine to carry out experiments, to alter behaviour, to train and correct individuals. Panopticism is a *general principle* applicable to all institutions throughout a country; it is not a dream building, but the diagram of a mechanism of power reduced to its ideal form.

Panopticism appears to be merely the solution of a technical problem; but through it a new type of society emerges, a society not of spectacle but of surveillance. This is done through the disciplines, those tiny, everyday, physical mechanisms, those systems of micropower that are essentially non-egalitarian and asymmetrical. The disciplines characterize, classify, specialize; they distribute along a scale, around a norm, hierarchize individuals in relation to one another and, if necessary, disqualify and invalidate.

Foucault: an appraisal

Foucault's work is an immensely valuable intervention — he has contributed greatly to our understanding of psychiatry, medicine, sexuality, law and discipline. He has written about these 'discourses' (systems of 'logic', chains of signs) in such a way that his readers can understand them as *practices*. I have outlined *one* of the threads to be found in Foucault's *Discipline and Punish* because I find his work insightful in the following ways:

First, though he does not fully expound his conception of the relation between knowledge and power, it does appear to be refreshingly different from the traditional accounts with which we are provided by the 'liberal' philosophers of education such as Richard Peters. In adopting a structuralist viewpoint, Foucault specifically rejects the humanist conception of the individual agent as the creator of knowledge: 'it is not the activity of the subject of knowledge ... but power-knowledge, the processes and struggles that traverse it and of which it is made up, that determines the forms and possible domains of knowledge'. Foucault suggests that we should abandon the belief that power makes mad and that the renunciation of power is one of the conditions of knowledge:[10]

> we should admit rather that power produces knowledge (and not simply by encouraging it because it serves power or by applying it because it is useful); that power and knowledge directly imply one another; that there is no power relation without the constitution of a field of knowledge, nor any knowledge that does not presuppose and constitute at the same time power relations.

Second, I find valuable Foucault's argument that schooling is a disciplinary mechanism. He argues that the extension of disciplinary institutions that occurred in the eighteenth century was only the most visible aspect of various, more profound processes. Whilst at first the disciplines had only a negative role, to neutralize dangers, they soon began to play a positive role: they functioned increasingly as techniques for making individuals not only *docile but useful*. As this was the period in which the new class power was developing, the 'disciplines' became attached to the most important and productive functions within society: the war machine, factory production, the transmission of knowledge, the diffusion of aptitudes and skills.

Now, the thesis that schooling consists of disciplinary mechanisms to render individuals docile but useful is also the view of the Americans Samuel Bowles and Herbert Gintis in their book, *Schooling in Capitalist America*. But what Foucault does is to provide the historical background to this argument by placing the beginnings of the disciplinary process in the eighteenth century. He puts the functions of the school in relationship to what was happening in other disciplinary institutions, military, medical, and industrial. It is clear that what concerned the disciplinary institutions was no longer the offence, the attack on 'the common interest', it was the departure from the norm that haunted the court, the asylum, the prison, the school.

We have seen in our time a tremendous growth of disciplinary institutions; ever more important powers have been given them, as medicine, psychology, public assistance, social work, education assume an increasing share of the powers of supervision and assessment. The mechanisms of normalization are becoming ever more rigorous in their application. Our institutions are intended to alleviate pain and suffering, to cure and comfort, yet they all tend, like the prison, to exercise a power of normalization. Foucault's work draws attention to the fact that the judges of normality are present everywhere:[11]

We are in the society of the teacher-judge, the doctor-judge, the educator-judge, the social-worker judge; it is on them that the universal reign of the normative is based; and each individual, wherever he may find himself, subjects to it his body, his gestures, his behaviour, his aptitudes, his achievements.

Foucault points to the fact that the failure of the prison has always been accompanied by its maintenance. What, he asks, is served by the failure of the prison? Prisons do not diminish the crime rate, they cannot fail to produce delinquents, and encourage recidivism. The true function of the prison is not to eliminate illegality, but to neutralize it; illegality is identified with what Foucault calls 'delinquency', a form of illegality that is pathologized, deprived of any political content, individualized. The prison creates an illegality which provides a rationale for a supervision of the entire society. Similarly, we could ask: what is served by the failure of the school? Just as prison, and no doubt punishment in general, is not intended to eliminate offences, but rather to distinguish them, to distribute them, to use them, so, perhaps, schools do not fulfil the function of education – they train pupils for docility and 'usefulness'.

Having stated some of the reasons why I consider Foucault's contribution to the study of the school to be valuable, I shall now make a few critical remarks about his work. One limitation is that Foucault studies the birth of the disciplinary institutions only in the French system. By not attempting a comparative examination, he neglects the analysis of important national differences in historical development and institutions. One wonders: to what extent is it possible to generalize from the French experience? Foucault stresses the characteristics that prisons, factories, barracks, hospitals and schools have in common, but perhaps it could be argued, just as adequately, that there are essential *differences* between schools and the other institutions. However, Foucault deliberately ignores these in his resolve to construct a trenchant critique of power.

Foucault asserts that most of the traditional theories (including Marxist ones) neglect the main problem about power: its *forms*. Forms of power are not reducible either to their *functions* (for example, that of reproducing relations of production) or to their *possession* (that is, to their being the property or instrument of a particular class). Thus the simple seizure of power by the working class, or the simple investment of existing forms of power with new functions in each case leaves the *forms* themselves untouched. A theory which considers the functions of power and neglects the forms is deficient. Similarly, a theory which directs attention exclusively to the class which wields power, and neglects the forms through which that class exercises its dominance is inadequate.

In short, Foucault argues that in most theories of power questions are usually limited to the nature of the functions or class interests rather than the disciplinary mode of domination itself. This is one of Foucault's main criticisms of Marxism. He sees in socialism merely a replication of the forms of power existing in the capitalist world. Foucault seems to have ignored the writings of Marx and Lenin in which they argued that the revolution does *not* merely consist in the transfer of power from one class to another, but in a transition from one form of power to another, the formation of new relations.[12] Foucault's point, however, is an important one. In education, for example, I know many socialists who see working-class pupils as being deprived, as having *less* knowledge than other classes. Their remedy, then, is that working-class kids should have *more* of the *same*. In other words, the form of education does not need to change — it just needs to be redistributed.

But what is Foucault's own conception of power? He is remarkably ambiguous. He insists that discipline may be identified neither with an institution nor with an apparatus; it is a type of power, a modality for the exercise of power, comprising a whole set of instruments, techniques, procedures, levels of application:[13]

> Power . . . is conceived not as a property but as a strategy, its effects of domination are attributed not to 'appropriation', but to dispositions, manoeuvres, tactics, techniques, functionings; one should decipher in it a network of relations, constantly in tension, in activity, rather than a privilege one might possess; one should take as its model a perpetual battle rather than a contract regulating a transaction or the conquest of a territory. In short this power is exercised rather than possessed; it is not the 'privilege', acquired or preserved, of the dominant class, but the overall effect of its strategic positions — an effect that is manifested and sometimes extended by the position of those who are dominated . . . This means that these relations go right down into the depths of society.

Foucault is arguing here against those theories that see power emanating from some central organizing entity such as the state. He contends that the over-emphasis on the state leaves unexplored the hidden nature of the 'disciplines'. It should be stressed that *the 'disciplines' are not things or institutions but forms of relation*. In his view, the disciplines are constituted not from above to below as if from some central organizing entity, but out of minute and diffuse relations. The conception of a unified power deriving from the state and of a unified struggle for the state must therefore be replaced by one of a multiplicity of power relations emerging from below and a multiplicity of 'resistances' engendered by them. This is why Foucault's writings have a great appeal to anti-authoritarians; against the particular mani-festations of disciplinary power he offers a new basis for the diverse and decentred struggles of prisoners, women, blacks, mental patients, welfare recipients, factory workers, and students.

For Foucault, power produces reality. Power appears as a constitu-tive subject, not exercised as something whose existence is independent of reality, but creating the very objects on which it is imposed. But if power is constitutive of reality, there is nothing outside of power, power can only appear as unconditioned. That is to say, what is offered as the basis of the emergence of the disciplines is simultaneously analysed as their effect. As a result he is unable to explain the emer-gence of different forms of power. But the crucial point is that Foucault's premise is incorrect; it is not the case that power produces reality. As Bob Fine has pointed out, *the exercise of power depends on material conditions existing independently of it*. In short, Foucault ignores the material conditions necessary for the construction and administration of 'panopticism'.[14]

Another weakness of Foucault's approach is that though he attacks the disciplines, he is relatively uncritical about the law. It could be said on Foucault's behalf that he provides a counterweight against those Marxists, like Pashukanis, who are highly critical of the bourgeois form of law but leave the forms of technical control unanalysed. As I mentioned earlier, Foucault concentrates on the proliferation of 'judges' who take the form of technical experts — teachers, doctors, psychologists, guards, social workers. As they operate in a sphere well protected from judicial or popular intervention, an antithesis has developed between discipline and democracy. Disciplinary power co-exists with democratic forms and undermines them from within. The roots of discipline are so deep in the organization of modern society that the subordination of discipline to democratic control is increas-ingly difficult.

Foucault locates the development of the disciplinary mechanisms in large-scale and productive industry. It is the technical requirements of mass production in industrial society, not capital, that is projected as the root of the disciplines. He rejects the class analysis of Marx which attempts to derive the existing forms of power from the productive relations of capitalist society. Marx showed in his analysis that it is the *capital* relation that established the necessity for a division of the supervised and the supervisors, for a structure of non-reciprocal obser-vation, judgment and punishment.

To summarize some of the criticisms of Foucault's work: I would argue that he makes such a blanket condemnation of the disciplines that he fails to see that the development of medicine, psychology, education must have made some useful contributions. He makes no reference to the positive aspects of discipline at all. Even in a socialist society some form of (self-)discipline — the realization of social obligations of members to each other — will be necessary.

Foucault's critique seems to be based not against a determinate form of social organization but against rational organization as such. Though it is evident that he is arguing only against certain forms, one gains the impression that Foucault's critique of discipline implies an opposition to all large-scale organization, to the 'rational' employment of labour, indeed to power itself.

Critical of the mechanistic view that asserts that the superstructure is determined by the economic base, Foucault persistently emphasizes the heterogeneity of discourses. He is greatly admired for his sophisticated non-reductionist accounts by many social scientists. However, I find that his stress on the multiplicity of power relations is such that it is difficult to utilize his theory of power in the analysis of a contemporary political situation. I think this is because there is a silence in his work about how things are connected together. As there is no centre of power, not even a network of forces, but a 'multiple network of diverse elements — walls, space, institution, rules, discourse, a strategic distribution of elements of different natures and levels', it is difficult to analyse a political conjuncture as a whole, a totality.[15] Moreover, there is little specific reference to the state. Though his study describes how 'disciplines' extended their various forms and covered the nation, he does not discuss the state in the eighteenth century and its contemporary development.

In short, Foucault's pessimistic analysis has the following limitations: his concept of power is inadequate, and the lack of explication of the concept of the state is a serious omission. Furthermore, he gives insufficient attention to the economic level; there is no analysis of capital. These criticisms are interconnected in that power cannot be separated from capital and the state. In my view, the growth of disciplinary institutions, the agencies of normalization, cannot be fully understood without a study of the increasing intervention of the capitalist state. But before I describe precisely why this is the case, it seems appropriate first to explore one of Foucault's themes. I propose to take a closer look at examinations and ranking. Examinations do establish over individuals a visibility through which they are differentiated and judged, but I want to relate the processes of assessment, teachers' marking, to the economy. The marking of teachers, the grading, does not only construct pupils' identities, it is also connected with the economic division of labour. It is now becoming clear that the educational system is concerned not only with disciplining the individuals but also with training and grading the future labour force.

School as a grading mechanism: teachers' marking

At one time we were told that education was 'preparation for life', but the rhetoric now increasingly being used is that it is 'preparation for work'. 'Education', broadly speaking, is usually associated with a liberal view of knowledge, a humanistic view of learning; 'schooling' is often connected with 'training', the performance of certain 'technical' functions. As the aim of manpower planners is to obtain a correspondence between the work of the school and the needs of industry, 'training' aspects are becoming increasingly dominant. In 1968, for example, John Vaizey made a declaration stressing that young people should have basic numeracy, literacy, some basic knowledge of science, and social skills. This theme has been taken up and the instilling of appropriate attitudes is now seen as an integral aspect of labour discipline. This requires categorization, assessment and grading.

Whilst the schools' career service focuses on guidance to individuals, the Manpower Services Commission represents a social approach to the problem of youth employment. A number of government-sponsored training schemes have been instituted to cope with rising youth unemployment. Many of these young people have a negative self-image, a sense of being determined by the social system. In most of the training schemes it is noticeable that subjects are still treated as discrete areas, and the skills that are taught are of a narrow sort. Even when the courses are innovative they usually follow only limited, reformist goals.

Unemployment has to some degree always existed in capitalism, but in the past it was projected as a problem associated with stereotypes of drunkenness, criminality, or some other 'pathological' factor. Now, gradually, a change in social perception is taking place. The perception has become based on an economic factor: unemployed people are those who have not been able to sell their labour power because of certain structural conditions. In such a context assessment through marking takes on an even more important function than in the past.

Marking is an important activity for teachers, they feel that they 'must keep up with it'. But though it is obvious and 'visible' it is largely an unresearched activity, long neglected by most sociologists and teachers. There are, of course, countless texts on the quantitative aspects, outlining various numerical procedures, their accuracy, reliability, etc., but they do not ask questions such as: What functions does evaluation have? What purposes does it serve and what social relations does it exemplify?

Let us begin by asking: What do the representations in a mark-book mean? What is it that people are doing when they mark? I would want to argue that pupils come to have identities attributed to them through teachers' marking. Once marking procedures, instruments and measures are provided, they come to be seen as neutral techniques rather than interpretative, socially constructed processes. In other words, methods of marking according to certain 'standards' come to be taken for granted, and these remain unquestioned. A pupil's career within the school is indicated by the mark-sheet. Gradually the record-cards and reports begin to influence the choice of subjects studied, and determine the examinations taken. Thus both teachers and pupils place themselves in a subordinate relation to certain 'standards' and knowledge become reified, separated from the knower. In this process, pupils are socialized into seeing grades as 'a return for work done' and their labour and its products as commodities.[16]

Through marking and grading, then, certain children are allowed access to certain subjects at certain levels, which are then tested. The examination qualifications gained are passports to various types of advanced, higher, and further education. Ideological elements of social hierarchy are also apparent in the structure of educational institutions to which the students go: colleges of further education, colleges of education, polytechnics, universities. The privileges and rewards that accrue from tertiary education can function as a means of gaining the allegiance of the socially mobile. Occupations are delineated in a certain way, the delineation itself being an ideological matter. The mental and manual division, the separation between head (managers) and hand (workers), is reinforced by qualifications. Entry qualifications are ideological in the sense that they are used to differentiate, hierarchize occupations. (And it should be remembered that hierarchies exist not only in 'academic' education, but also in other types. I often wonder why nurses cannot study a few more course units to qualify as doctors.)

In industry, techniques such as job-evaluation, measured-time work, method-time measurement and the like are used. These techniques are designed by management to reverse the collective sale of the commodity of labour-power (which is the justification for the existence of the trade unions) by individualizing wages, in other words, by fragmenting wage-earners once more and reintroducing competition into their ranks. It is my contention that analogous techniques are used in schools to differentiate students by the emphasis on individualism and competition. A hierarchical educational system necessarily implies less privileged workers. And so we see, on the one hand, a movement towards even higher qualifications and, on the other, a mass process of (deskilled) training. Thus the division between mental and manual labour is reproduced.

My argument in this section is simple enough: teachers' marking, a bridging process between informal and formal procedures of assessment, affects pupils' careers in school and life. The activity of marking is inevitably influenced by class, gender and ethnic categories. Educational categories create occupations within the social division of labour. For these reasons, much more research needs to be done on such questions as: Who assesses whom? Why? And for whose interest? I suggest that we should shift our attention from psychologistic questions such as 'How do teachers assess?' to social questions such as 'What function does assessment serve?' Of course, it will be argued that if teachers cannot or do not assess children, 'they can't really be teaching effectively'. The 'liberal philosophers', particularly, stress this view: they point out that assessment can be done only in relation to certain standards, and that they should be precisely indicated to children. And so there is a stress on 'objective' tests, and their moderation; It is not readily admitted that emphasis on 'standards' leads to conventional, convergent forms of thinking. It is never made clear why most assessments are based on notions of individual competition rather than collective work. And, of course, it is never asked: Whose standards are being used and why?

An individual teacher may see her marking as having only a motivational purpose, but education is much more than the conscious intentions of the people who work in it; structurally, it can be seen as a form of social control. Schooling is basically to do with the production of the commodity labour power and teachers are involved in its categorization.

As stated above, the argument that the main functions of education are the training of manpower and the reproduction of capitalist social relations, sounds like a functionalist explanation. Structural functionalism, particularly in the United States of America, has been linked with an ideological position: an emphasis on the preservation of stability and the *status quo*, a stress on conservatism and consensus politics. Now, if we adopt a functionalist explanation of the link between education and industry, there are some problems that must be recognized. First, it is reductionist to perceive the educational system as a unitary system, without contradictions. Second, structural functionalists stress the 'needs' of the social system, but does not a Marxist approach need to differentiate itself from a functionalist point of view? What, in other words, is the difference between Right functionalism (Parsons) and Left functionalism?[17]

This raises a fundamental question about the role of education: What should be the relationship between schools and industry? This is a problem not only for the political Right, which stresses the convergence of interests between industry and education, but also for the Left. There has always been some relation, but what precisely should it be now — and in a future socialist society? Third, if one emphasizes schooling, 'training for work', one has to explain the relationship between this 'function' and the 'dysfunctions'. How is one to explain the emphasis on training when an increasing number of occupations and services, mostly in the public sector, do not produce surplus value? Why is 'training' being given when jobs, particularly for young school leavers, are not available? To answer these questions we shall have to look at the nature of work under capitalism.

In this chapter I have focussed on those aspects of Foucault's work that relate specifically to the school; how discipline operates the following techniques: the organization of space, the new economy of time, the training for obedience, the notion of exercise in 'the educational programme', the role of examinations, and coercion by surveillance. Foucault's thesis was stressed because he challenges our presuppositions. It is so often taken for granted that medicine, law, social work, education are the 'helping' professions that we forget that these 'service industries' are also concerned with normalization. These 'caring' professions (note how they redefine certain conditions as problems, categories of deficiency) can also be seen as agencies that exercise power; they enforce discipline.

It has been argued that the school is a disciplinary and grading mechanism. Schools child-mind, skill, discipline and grade the workforce. But as both teachers and pupils are highly differentiated there are many different outcomes; in some classrooms there is passivity, in others resistance. But in both, marking, which seems such an individualistic activity, is related to the division of labour. Marking, grading, assessment, evaluation — these activities should not be isolated from the political-economic relations of capitalism within which schooling is situated. From this it follows that the provision of more 'opportunities' in education cannot do much to alter present inequalities. The determinants of inequality are outside the terrain of education.

Having discussed in this chapter the view that the school is a disciplinary institution, I now want to move on to a discussion of another form of discipline: the capitalist labour process, the changes taking place within it, and its effects.

Chapter 3

The emphasis on work-socialization

Schooling for industry

One of the main features of monopoly capitalism is the increasing use of mechanization and automation, the use of electronics and micro-processors. As I explained in the last chapter, capital's relentless compulsion to technologize expels more and more workers from the productive process, forcing them to join the ranks of the 'reserve army of labour', the unemployed. Youth employment has been especially affected by current changes in the labour process. As there is a decline in the demand for unskilled manual workers a large proportion of the unemployed are young school-leavers.

The problem of youth unemployment is connected with many fears that are not usually explicitly stated. There is, for example, an underlying fear of social and political unrest.[1] First, could the young unemployed become so disaffected that they become a threat to existing authority structures? Second, there is a concern about the discrepancy between the purposes of the educational system and the needs of industry. There seems to be a mismatch between the qualities of young people turned out by the schools and the qualities of young people required by industry. How is this gap going to be bridged? Third, there is a disquiet amongst employers about a possible skill shortage in the future. At the moment, because of the current crisis, there is a cutting back in training, but what is going to happen in the future when there is an upturn in the economy and a larger supply of skilled labour is needed? Fourth — a related point — there is an anxiety about future employability. If young people begin to lose their 'motivation', their desire to be good, responsible workers, what is going to happen when jobs eventually become available? Employers are becoming increasingly aware that if young people are spending several years waiting in the dole queue, they are no longer experiencing 'work discipline'. Could the culture of wagelessness amongst youth develop into *a refusal of all work*? Indeed, some youth groups such as 'skinheads', 'punks', 'rockers', 'Rastas' (with their associated musical forms) can be seen as a cultural response, a form of resistance, to the conditions young people face.[2]

Youth unemployment, then, is a serious problem for the state for many reasons. It actually threatens the ideological notion that schooling is a good thing. If after 'fifteen thousand hours' at school there is no job, the usefulness of schooling, and the nature of society, will be increasingly questioned.[3] Young people wasting their lives on the street doing *nothing* because they have no money, no responsibility, no influence, may well become disaffected.[4] And, of course, unemployment connects with other areas of exploitation: many of the wageless are children of manual workers. They are often black and suffer from many forms of discrimination. As we shall see, many of these youngsters rejected school as an irrelevant imposition.

Some of the attempts to 'remedy' the situation are well known. The schools are beginning to emphasize certain aspects of the curriculum, for example, the inculcation of (precisely defined) skills.[5] There is also a shift towards more vocational courses; 'industrial relevance' is being stressed now in the universities. And, allied with this, there is an increasing emphasis on career advice, work-experience, work-*socialization*. To confront the problems of youth unemployment, new institutions, quasi-autonomous government organizations, such as the Manpower Services Commission have been set up.[6] Job-creation schemes, youth opportunity programmes have been devised. These schemes help to 'reduce' unemployment figures; they 'rotate' the unemployed, but do they really prepare the labour force or are they merely palliatives?

I would argue that though employers say that industry's needs are not being met, what is really meant is that only workers with certain attitudes (rather than technical knowledge) are required: compliant, adaptable, mobile workers. The Holland Report stressed work training, yet many of these schemes are not about teaching craft skills, but about work-socialization. This is seen most clearly in further education colleges where there has been a move towards a psychologistic stress in the teaching of so-called 'communication-skills'.

It is ironic that this emphasis on vocational training is occurring precisely at a time when job opportunities for most young people are limited. In the past, teachers exhorted their pupils to 'work hard and pass their exams' but this has little credence for students now who realize that they will probably be unemployed; they know that less labour is required as industries rapidly adopt computerized technology. Questions about the curriculum, therefore, are increasingly about school-work relations, and obviously these contradictions will increasingly affect the way in which teachers are perceived.

It is noticeable that in the media the inherent weaknesses, the contradictions of capitalism are never discussed – they become transformed into discrete, manageable, dysfunctions such as 'the problem of unemployment'. Faced with such a crisis, how does social-democratic ideology attempt to defuse the situation? First, unemployment is presented, in the media and elsewhere, as a moral issue. There are two common attitudes: the 'hard' approach asserts that the young unemployed 'must learn to live in the real world', they must get up on time, be punctual, develop good habits, learn to accept discipline, gain 'work-experience'. The 'soft' version defines the problem in psychological terms; the focus is on the personal troubles rather than the social problem. The unemployed school-leaver is said to lack communication skills; s/he is said to be having a difficult time because of conflicting parental values and other pressures. Education for leisure is often involved. Neither approach discusses the crisis as the logical outcome of the contradictions within the capitalist economy.

A complex restructuring is taking place within capitalism, which includes the proletarianization of the professions and a deskilling of labour. There is no longer a demand for casual, unskilled manual work and there are now redundancies even amongst skilled workers – often a permanent loss of employment. Changes in the labour process are leading to changes in quantity and quality of labour power required by capital. These are some of the themes of Harry Braverman's influential book *Labour and Monopoly Capitalism*.[7] I shall be arguing that the education system in its role as producer and organizer of labour power is responding (though slowly and unevenly) to the changing economic conditions. In order to understand better the restructuring that is taking place, it is first necessary to consider Braverman's argument.

The labour process: an exposition

Traditional sociology has long neglected the study of the nature of work but this subject is central to Braverman who begins by asking: What is work? Drawing on Marx, he states that work is an essentially human activity; human beings are uniquely capable of deliberately acting upon and changing the world – they have the power of conceptual thought, of imagination. Work is good, it realizes human spontaneity and has the highest potential value. And yet work is coercive; this is not because of its nature, but because of the historical conditions under which it is performed, the way in which it has to be performed under capitalism.

Braverman traces historically how the labour process has come to be controlled by capitalism. At one time there were sub-contractors and craft organizations, but with the coming of industrialization there were new developments: workers had to work regular hours under one factory roof. Capitalism subdivided work within an industry; operations were separated and done by different people so that workers could not complete a process. Thus the division of labour in the workshop began to destroy many occupations: workers became deskilled.

Braverman focuses on Frederick Taylor and others who applied the methods of science on behalf of management. The science of management directs the way and the speed at which the work has to be performed. The three main characteristics of management are these: First of all, management gathers and tabulates all traditional knowledge. There is then a separation between conception and execution, between mental and manual labour, the former directing the latter. Third, management acquires a monopoly of knowledge. Science, itself bought and sold like any other commodity, becomes incorporated into capitalism. As control is taken away from the workers, they become interchangeable. Braverman concentrates on analysing changes in the labour process in the new service occupations, such as office work.[8] He argues that office work, routinized, mechanically paced paper-processing, is now similar to manual work in the factory.

But what causes the restructuring that is taking place? Capital, to increase its profits, attempts to increase productivity of labour by the use of more machinery and advanced technology. (This theme will be fully developed in later chapters of this book.) For Braverman, then, the main features of labour under monopoly capitalism are the atrophy of skill, the degradation of work, and the dehumanization of human beings.

There are two basic managerial strategies: responsible autonomy and direct control. The direct control strategy tries to control labour by means of tight supervision and by minimizing individual worker responsibility through the use of Taylorist techniques. This strategy treats workers as machines, and writers who focus on it emphasize that with deskilling there is a homogenization of the proletariat and that management creates spurious hierarchies so as to 'divide and rule' the working class. Braverman, the most sophisticated of the writers who use this approach, is obviously inspired by a humanistic Marxism. This accounts for several interesting features in his work.

First, Braverman's book is a criticism not only of direct control but also of responsible autonomy strategy, which attempts to give workers status, autonomy, and responsibility so as to try to win their loyalty ideologically, in a manner beneficial to the firm.[9] Second, Braverman is critical of those vulgar Marxists who believe that because

33

there is an increasing proletarianization there is some sort of automatic politicization. He is sceptical of such a view because it assumes a certain homogeneity in the working class. And, third, he challenges the narrow technicist view prevalent in Russia. He is critical of industrialization in the Soviet Union where the productive forces have been vastly developed but the relations of production, that is to say, the relations between *people*, have not radically changed.[10] It is a society in which workers, as yet, do not have direct control, where the division between intellectual and manual labour has not been abolished.

A discussion of Braverman's thesis

The main theme of *Labour and Monopoly Capitalism* is the degradation of craft-work into deskilled labour. The worker is subordinated to the imperatives of capital accumulation which has two aims. The first of these is to cheapen labour; complex labour is substituted by simple labour, which means that skill requirements are incessantly lowered. The second aim is to capture effective capitalist control of the labour process. In destroying craft as a process under the control of the worker, the capitalist reconstitutes it as a process under his own control. He dictates each step of the process, including its mode of performance. Thus the labour process is dominated and shaped by the accumulation of capital. Now, whilst this is broadly true, it should be said that Braverman has a rather idealized conception of craft-work. The 'artisan ideal' leads him to neglect the fact that as well as deskilling when new processes are utilized, (some) reskilling, or the learning of new skills, is also involved. There have been cases in which a 'skill' has been artificially created by the workers themselves in a formerly 'unskilled' occupation.

Braverman writes of the United States, and there is an ambiguity about whether his work applies only to that particular social formation or whether, because capitalism is a world system, it applies universally. It has been found that in the nineteenth century, for instance, British and American capital adopted different strategies. The adoption of 'scientific management' was uneven; whilst the United States was a pioneer of Taylorism, in Europe the introduction of scientific management was retarded (until the First World War) because of the existence of lower wages and the cushion of imperialism. This illustrates the problem (to be discussed later in the book) that if one works at the most general and abstract level of 'the logic of capital', as some theorists do, it is sometimes difficult to integrate it with a concrete analysis at the empirical, historical level.

Braverman's thesis, in short, is that craft expertise has been destroyed and has been replaced by capitalist control of the labour process. It is not often fully realized that Taylorism had a significant *ideological* role in that it undermined a 'populist' conception of labour as the creative agent and substituted a conception of labour as a passive factor in production. Whilst Braverman retains the former, the populist craft conception, his thesis is itself imbued with the latter, a passive view of the working class. His conceptualization of the working class is as if it was weak and passive, there is little reference to working-class resistance and struggle. The capacity of capital to reorganize the labour process, to degrade workers and expel them to a less mechanized sector, is so heavily emphasized that capitalism appears as an all-powerful juggernaut. For Braverman, capitalist control and domination is secured within production; the degradation of work and the disciplining effect of the reserve army of labour produce a passive and inert working class: a shrinking elite of conceptualizers confront a mass of deskilled labourers. In such a view, the working class as an active agency is forgotten.

Furthermore, whilst Braverman notes the influence of economistic trade unionism (that which stresses wage increases and turns away from the struggle for political change), he neglects the broader ideological and political conditions of capitalist hegemony. He leaves out the state and its interventions in reconstructing class relations. Capital is totally dominant; the relationship between capital and the role of the state (the attempt of the latter to deal with massive unemployment for example) is hardly discussed.

Finally, it could be said that Braverman's work ignores the contradictions and struggles which beset mechanization in the form of the tendency of the rate of profit to fall and the counter-tendencies.[11] Because of these weaknesses in Braverman's account, he is unable to address the complex, uneven and contradictory character of the organization of collective labour.

In spite of these criticisms, Braverman's work is of considerable significance. Though he does not deal directly with education, I think that one of the ways in which his account is valuable is that it makes us aware of the need to develop an *analysis of the labour process within education*. The following brief suggestions only point towards some of the areas in which research needs to be undertaken.

(a) *The division between mental/manual labour in the educational system and within schools*

One of the procedures being used to exert greater control is systems management. This is a successor of Taylor's scientific management but its purpose is the same: the separation of conception from execution.[12] Head teachers in many areas now have to attend management courses, and have supported this tendency as it increases their professional status. The split between administrative/bureaucratic management and practising class teachers is thus widening in schools. The growth of specialization in mental labour has led bureaucrats to prefer managerial solutions, but these only displace the main problem. Status once depended on 'mystique' but is now being replaced by a technical notion of skills. The same fragmentation and routinization that is taking place in production is also occurring in teaching.

(b) The managerial practices in educational institutions that parallel those in industry

Certain management practices, which exemplify an anti-collectivism (postal ballots, for example), are being increasingly imitated in educational institutions.

(c) The fragmentation and atomization of the teaching labour force

Common procedures include the following: there is a strengthening of hierarchization in large schools through differentials. The individuals of a group that has a strong ideological identity are separated and then merged into a larger organization. The time that teacher/workers are in group contact with one another is minimized (for example, short lunch periods, etc.).

In short, all these processes, the increase of 'rationalization' and 'cost-effectiveness' in education, demonstrate the spread of capitalist principles. We need to know in what areas of teachers' work, and in what manner, are the managerial strategies of direct control and responsible autonomy being used in schools. To what extent does this management orientation suppress the possibility of other approaches which would involve planning for human needs and purposes?

From school to manual work: a cultural view

In contrast with Braverman's economic analysis, some writers have reacted by making a plea for an analysis of work from a *cultural* point of view. Paul Willis, for example, has argued this in his studies of working-class youth and their transition from school to work.[13] He is particularly interested in the culture that the 'lads' bring to the workplace. Work, he argues, must occupy a central place in any full sense of culture. After all, the main reality for most people for most of the time is work; they base their identities on *work* activities, and are defined by others essentially through their relation to work. Work makes us and is made by us.

Willis's study of 'how working-class kids get working-class jobs' begins with a consideration of the schooling of disaffected youth.[14] He correctly points out that the struggle over authority in schools is really a fight between cultures. The struggle is between the formal and the informal, the school and the counter-school culture, the lads and the conformist 'ear'oles'. The lads attempt to limit the demands of the institution in various ways. The school is basically a place where the lads can have fun with their mates; 'having a laff' is important to them, and so is smoking, drinking, fighting, buying clothes, going out with girls. The lads are aggressive, racist, and sexist; they want excitement, but shortage of cash is a big problem.

The 'lads' reject institutionalized knowledge and the idea of qualifications. The possibility of real upward mobility seems so remote to them as to be meaningless. They want to live *now*, in the immediate present. There seems to be a sort of *cultural self-preparation* of the lads for a certain kind of work, and Willis argues that it is the school which has built up a certain resistance to mental work and the inclination to manual work. Mental work for 'the lads' is not only barred because of their particular experience in the school, but also because it is regarded as effeminate. There is, then, an urge to escape from school and to work in the real adult world. They know they are bound to a future of generalized labour. The 'lads' do not choose a 'career' or a particular job; as all unskilled manual work is the same, it does not matter what one does. The specific job is obtained quite randomly, by chance.

But after a while the lads' confidence and exhilaration at doing a man's job is followed by disillusion. Satisfaction or personal meaning was never expected from work. Once in the factory, it is found that the culture of the shop floor has many similarities with the counter-school culture which they have just left. The days begin to seem interminable, the weeks the same. Leisure is a false promise, and soon the lads realize they are trapped. The shopfloor becomes a prison, and education is seen retrospectively, and hopelessly, as the only escape. But by the time the answers are known it is too late to apply them.

The lads have a notion of authority relations, 'them and us', which actually accomplishes a recognition of, and an accommodation to, the existence of the power of employers and their enforcement of hierarchy. The lads 'stand up for themselves', but only in a restricted mode. How does this occur? The surprising thing is that shopfloor culture has some of the same determinants as, and marked similarities with, counter-school culture. Willis has perceived at least five elements in working-class 'culture of work'.

One of the main characteristics is the numbing sense of boredom and meaninglessness — how time drags at work. For most people work is dead time, human time sold for the possibility of a real life later. Yet, in spite of this, people do look for meaning, they do want to exercise their abilities; Willis remarks on the sheer mental and physical bravery of surviving in hostile conditions. There are still many rough, unpleasant, physically demanding jobs, and the basic attitudes and values developed in such jobs are still very important. There is a pride and self-esteem in doing a hard job well; but in such a job strength and bravery are expressed through masculinity and male chauvinism.

The second element in shopfloor culture is the attempt to gain informal control of the work process. By this Willis is referring to fiddling and 'winning materials', control of manning and the spread of production, the limitation of output. The third aspect of this culture is its distinctive form of language use, its (intimidatory) humour. A further important element of the shopfloor (and in the working class generally) is the belief that practice is more important then theory. Practical ability always comes first and is a condition of other kinds of knowledge. To put this in another way, theory is only useful if it really does help to do things (to accomplish practical tasks and change nature). This is in contrast with the bourgeois view that associates theory with qualifications, the power to be socially mobile — theory as a ticket to travel, to move upwards.

Another element in shopfloor culture is the articulation of manual labour power with assertive male-gender definitions. There is the irony that as work has been emptied of significance, this has been replaced with a transformed patriarchy. Manual labour is associated with the superiority of masculinity, it is suffused with aggressive qualities, machismo. Mental labour is associated with the social inferiority of femininity. A form of patriarchy, then, buttresses the mental/manual division of labour. Thus 'discontent with work is hinged away from a political discontent and confused in its proper logic by a huge detour into the symbolic sexual realm.'[15]

Willis concludes by noting that union officials and shop stewards can mobilize the 'lads', who express their anger and opposition very effectively in the *short* term, but longer-term objectives cannot be conceptualized in this way. The masculine style of confrontation demands an appropriate and honourable resolution, there must be visible and immediate concessions. But short-term, visible, dramatic concessions gained by workers in this way do not change any of the basic arrangements of the capitalist mode of production. Through these dramatic concessions hard cash can be won, but the wage packet may actually conceal longer-term defeats over the less visible issues of control and ownership.

For the 'lads' the (short-term) celebration of masculinity in labour power thus ends in long-term accommodation. Willis's work shows us how subordinate roles came to be taken on freely, how a segment of the working class reproduces its own submission. There is, then, an element of self-domination in the acceptance of subordinate roles in Western capitalism; an unfree condition is entered freely. In this process it is the state school that is a central case of mediated class conflict and of class reproduction.

Some Comments on *Learning to Labour*

Willis, in contrast to Braverman's economic analysis, gives a cultural account and, at the same time, attempts to integrate the ideological and economic levels. Whilst in Braverman there is little reference to resistance, Willis goes to the other extreme; his emphasis on resistance seems to be exaggerated. Willis writes of 'the massive attempt to gain informal control of the work process'. He mentioned 'fiddling', 'winning materials', 'ostracism', and the fact that 'in many plants the men, themselves, to all intents and purposes actually control at least manning and the speed of production'. But what does all this amount to? At the end Willis has to concede that what has developed is merely 'trade union consciousness'.

Willis attempts to show how occupational positions and the cultural attributes of working-class subordination appear to be chosen rather than imposed, but like the lads he is writing about, he gets himself into a fix. On the one hand, he greatly admires the agency of the lads, he continually stresses their rationality and creativity:[16]

> By penetrating the contradiction at the heart of the working-class
> school the counter-school culture helps to liberate its members
> from the burden of conformism and conventional achievement . . .
> Getting through a term without putting pen to paper, the continu-
> ous evasion of the teacher's authority, the guerilla warfare of the
> classroom and corridor is partly about limiting such demands upon
> the self.

But what sort of liberation is this? I suggest that in Willis's contribution to the theory of reproduction of class-divided society there is a tendency to exaggerate and romanticize (the counter-school and) working-class culture. Willis relies so heavily, theoretically and methodologically, on ethnography, the lads' own version of their biography, that when in his account the lads have become trapped in their unskilled jobs, he cannot then criticize their rationality. He cannot explicitly bring himself to say that the lads' thinking was incorrect, that they acted foolishly. Of course, we do not know how *typical* this small group of white lads is, we do not know the effects of different mediations such as sex and race. But is there really nothing the lads could have done to avoid their own damnation? It is a pity that Willis neglects to study the 'ear'oles', who were conformist in terms of school culture, but may yet have a potentiality for developing a radical consciousness greater than the more obviously disaffected lads. Nor does the author say anything about the teachers, which is regrettable, because they have an important and contradictory role in a state apparatus. At the pessimistic conclusion, however, Willis states that 'it must be agreed that it is a condition for working-class development that working-class kids do develop certain disciplined skills in expression and symbolic manipulation.'[17] This must surely be one of the most urgent tasks facing socialist teachers.

Training for unemployment

In this chapter I have suggested that youth unemployment can only be fully explained by an understanding of the changes occurring in the economic system. Unemployment must be studied in the context of the objective *contradictions* that exist within the capitalist mode of production. In order to comprehend the complex restructuring that is taking place, we examined the labour process.

It is a common assumption amongst industrialists, politicians, and educationalists (of both Left and Right), that modern industrial development requires an increasingly skilled workforce and that schools and colleges are failing to provide it. Now, one of the reasons for the importance of Braverman is this: he challenges the widespread and *false* assumption that industry demands ever more highly skilled personnel in the labour force. For the mass of workers their skill does not only fall in an absolute sense, in that they lose craft and traditional abilities without gaining new abilities adequate to compensate the loss, but it falls even more in a relative sense. The more science is incorporated into the labour process, the less the worker understands it; intelligence is extracted out of labour's control and concentrated on the side of capital, represented by management and machines.

To say this in another way, even though there is an apparent move towards employers demanding more and higher qualifications, the real skill content of most factory work is getting less. What employers need in general is a less skilled workforce which is flexible enough to allow interchange between standardized processes.

But this is not readily admitted; this is not how things are made to appear — we are told that 'schools are failing'. Gramsci's concept of hegemony is useful here in explaining why this shift of focus has come about.[18] Hegemony refers to a situation in which an alliance of social groups exerts authority over subordinate groups not simply by the direct imposition of ruling ideas but by winning and shaping consent. As hegemony is not universal or permanent, it has to be continually won, sustained, reproduced. Now, the theme that 'schools are failing' has been taken up and constantly publicized during the last few years, and I would contend that this shift of focus and responsibility on to the schools is an attempt to re-form public opinion, *to shape consent* for new definitions and policies that restructure school-work relations at a time of deepening recession.

Broadly, there are two main criticism of schools: it is said that many of the subjects studied, especially at the more advanced stages, are not directly useful or relevant to the economy; there are too many courses in the arts and the social sciences and too few in the natural sciences, mathematics, engineering and technology. Secondly, it is said that students are not reaching high enough levels in the subjects that they are studying, standards being particularly low in numeracy and literacy.[19] Industrialists in particular have blamed the schools for declining standards and have often linked this, as I suggested in Chapter 1, with an attack on 'progressivism'. Schools are being reproached for their 'lack of contact with industry', a lack of knowledge of industry's needs. School-leavers, it is said, 'don't know what work is about'. In this context, government training schemes and programmes can be seen as a form of work-socialization by the state for capital.

To say this in a different way, there is a demand that schools and training programmes become the source of the work ethic. Listen to the tone of voice of the careers teacher speaking to the fifth-year 'lads': 'I've told you before, bad habits at school take a lot of throwing over. If you're resentful of authority here, and have a bad attitude towards discipline, it will carry on at work, it will show there, and they won't have time for it.' Paul Willis has pointed out how the conformist values of the workplace are brought back into the school; this often takes the form of a blackmail which says both that 'If you are not developing the right attitudes now, you will not succeed at work', and also more practically, 'If you do not co-operate now, you will not get a good leaving report.'[20]

To recapitulate: what employers are really anxious about are not standards of literacy and numeracy at all, but young people's *attitudes*. The young are seen as lacking certain acceptable 'social values' such as willing acceptance of factory discipline and hierarchy.[21] And so one response to young people's questioning of authority, discipline, and the competitive spirit is the inculcation of these values, the increased emphasis on work-socialization through the apparatuses of the state. What employers want is a labour force that is adaptable and flexible, workers who are willing to continually retrain and to be occupationally mobile. Above all, capital requires labour that is co-operative and compliant.

But in spite of the exhortations of careers teachers and industrialists the work ethic is difficult to instil because most young people have an understanding of the boring, routine, repetitive, tedious nature of industrial work. Many of them are keenly aware of the developments in the new technology, they know that it does not always get rid of boring work; indeed, as the output becomes standardized, work becomes more monotonous. And it is now more carefully monitored, there is 'built-in' supervision.[22] But questions are beginning to be asked. What technology should we have? Couldn't technology be redesigned to serve the interests of everyone? My own view is that, as technology embodies the social relations in which it exists, there could be machines that increase productivity without deskilling people, machines that are designed in such a way that they could be controlled by workers, who are involved in *socially* useful production. In my experience, young women and men increasingly feel that technology must be the result of decisions that people make about how *society* should be organized.

This chapter has examined the emergence of the capitalist labour process; the next chapter will focus on the increasing role of the state. There has been a massive increase in state education since the 1870s. This historic change is a restructuring of power, a transformation in the relationship between education and the state. Does state education increase equality or does it actually reproduce and legitimate inequalities?

Chapter 4

Schooling and the state

Introduction

An understanding of the role of the state has become central to any sociological analysis of power in society. It is particularly important to try to understand the increasing intervention by the state in the education system. The main theoretical problem to be examined in this chapter is exemplified in the well-known remark made by Robert Lowe in 1867 after the town workers obtained the vote: 'We must educate our masters.' How do we make sense of this? Is this a call for state intervention, an opportunity for the working class to realize fully its educational potential, or does it refer to a new strategy, a subtle means of control, a way of 'gentling the masses'? The institutionalization of state education could, of course, be *both*, a strategy for providing the basic skills required for capitalist industrial expansion and yet, at the same time, an ideological instrument for socializing the workforce, for schooling the proletariat.

The introduction of compulsory education has improved the standard of working-class education in several ways, but I want to go on to say that this has been used ideologically to give the impression that 'the state works for the good of all!' Here is an example of the process by which the state presents an appearance of itself as being neutral, above the conflicts of antagonistic 'groups' and classes. I want to claim that the historical development of state education illustrates how apparent improvements, welfare reforms, actually disguise a process of co-optation, the recuperation of the working class.

To begin to understand how the determinants of inequality in education lie outside the educational system we will have to investigate the precise articulation between education, economy and the state. Is education a service for people or is it a tool of the state machine? One of the main problems in this area is that there seems to

43

be no simple or agreed definition of what the state is or how it should be analysed. There are differing conceptualizations of the state, but, as yet, we have no fully developed theory. We know very little about what the state is, what it does, and the precise relationship between state and capital. There is a danger that, if the state is conceived of in a unitary, homogeneous way, then it could lead to reductionism, to a false over-simplification. If, on the other hand, contradictions are allowed, then there is a necessity for a deeper analysis to discover the conditions, possibilities, and limits of state action. In the present chapter *each section represents a particular view of the relation between education and the state*. It is suggested that the 'liberal' view of education contains the assumptions that existing power arrangements are legitimate, and that the state is neutral. Then, in contrast, a Marxist viewpoint is presented through the work of Bowles and Gintis; they have argued that education, as it is constituted at the moment, serves the interest of capital. The chapter concludes with a discussion of the struggle to create an independent, working-class educational system, a strategy which was gradually replaced by the demand for educational provision through the state. This shift had immense, contradictory consequences. But, first, let us begin by considering briefly the origins of state provision of education in the nineteenth century, and the differences between 'minority' and 'mass' schooling.

Mass schooling: minority culture

One of the most important contributions to our understanding of schooling has been made by historians of education. Uncovering 'official' establishment history, they have demonstrated the difference between private, minority education, supported by the bourgeoisie, and the mass schooling provided for the working-class. At the beginning of the nineteenth century, industrialists trained children from the workhouse; then, as laws were passed against children being exploited in factories, the state began to provide, and gradually increase, school provision.[1] The schools of the working class were organized like factories: there was an emphasis on order, subordination, habits of industry and punctuality. Obedience and respect for authority, essential for the reproduction of an hierarchical society, was rigorously enforced. This was done by teachers who had themselves been socialized into seeing their role as being providers of character-training and pastoral care. As teachers they had a missionary function, a civilizing mission.

The process of institutionalized learning/socialization, now taken for granted as if it was 'natural', was an entirely new one. At one time children acquired their knowledge of how to live from their parents — as many children in the Third World still do today. There was no separation between family and work. What is new with the development of capitalism is the growth of importance of the school as the principal institution mediating between the world of the home and the world of work; there developed, gradually, the common belief that 'education' only occurs in schools. We have seen how this institution, this apparatus, has gradually increased its power: not only does it contain its inmates for longer and longer periods of time, but it is also the main channel for certificated entry into most occupations. In short, as the church has declined, school has become the dominant ideological state apparatus.[2]

In contrast with mass education, minority education is associated not with a vocation, a training for a job, but with *liberal education*, the development of the person; it stresses the importance of duty, self-discipline, responsibility and leadership. The liberal view of education emphasizes the importance of individualism, competition and rewards — for the winners. In this 'paradigm' certain attributes like intellectual capacity are stressed. Intellectual capacity is seen as if it was a natural category (like height), biological rather than social. Emphasis is placed on the early recognition of the capacity of 'gifted' children and their individual performance. The stress on the individual shifts the focus of concern away from societal problems and solutions to the realm of the psychological. This could be called a 'free-market' model of education but, like the so-called 'free market', it acts within certain rather limited parameters.

The parameters are taken for granted: often noticed but rarely questioned. They are those of hierarchy; the examinations which students take, the educational institutions which they attend, and the knowledge which they are taught there, are all ranked hierarchically in a way that mirrors the society outside. What is not yet fully recognized is that the concept of individual intelligence is not a universal notion but a historical one. It emerged in the nineteenth century with the division of labour. For the first time millions of workers were forced to sell their labour power for a wage on the 'free market', and in this context their 'capacities' were categorized, measured, quantified.[3]

Another important characteristic of the liberal view of education is its stress on high culture. This is a *tradition* which has a long history; it forms a powerful anti-egalitarian pressure group even today. Concisely, it believes that Western civilization is a precious heritage created over centuries by highly gifted individuals. This culture must be protected from the onslaught of the uneducated masses by the elite, a group who are above mere class interests. Inevitably, this tradition tends to be associated with a scepticism of modern industry and science, as it has a nostalgia for the cultural harmony, the stable (mythical) good society of the past. The leading exponents of this view are T.S. Eliot and F.R. Leavis.[4] I have outlined this position because of its continuing influence, as we shall see, on education.

The liberal view of education and the state

In most of the traditional 'establishment' textbooks three views of education are usually presented.

1 Education is said to be concerned with the 'initiation into the "forms" of knowledge'. This is the viewpoint propagated by the 'liberal' philosophers of education such as Richard Peters.

2 It is said that education is (primarily) for the full development of the individual. Progressivism, with its stress on pupil-centredness, is usually included in this category.

3 It is held that education is for equipping individuals for the 'needs' of society. Supporters of this view are to be found amongst the political Left and Right. Right-wing theorists usually base their views on the assumption that Britain is a democracy. Parliamentary representation is seen as the index of democracy; freedom, then, is defined in relation to the political sphere – the economic sphere being ignored.

It is generally assumed in the traditional textbook that 'tensions' can exist between these differing conceptions of education, but it is never conceded that political, *class* struggles about the definition of education are continually taking place. This can be clearly seen in the work of the 'liberal' philosphers of education. Broadly speaking, the liberal philosophers of education believe that education is concerned with knowledge for its own sake; they are extremely critical of 'progressive' education, and they have been remarkably silent about the pressure to gear education to the needs of industry. The aims of education, and educational policies, are seen primarily as *moral* matters. This is allied to the notion that society is made up of the *individuals* that constitute it. The aim of education, therefore, is to produce morally good individuals. This said, the liberal philosophers retire to the cave to clarify conceptual problems such as the meaning of the good life.

Embedded in the writings of the theorists who propagate the liberal view of education is a theory of the state. Not surprisingly, the theory happens to be the dominant one in society: democratic pluralism. This theory is based on the assumption that power in Western societies is competitive, fragmented, and diffuse; everybody directly or through organized interest groups has some power and no one has or can have too much, as evidenced by universal suffrage, free and regular elections, right to free speech, association and opposition, etc. In this model, competition between 'veto-groups' is sanctioned and guaranteed by the state, ensuring a 'balance of power'.

Implicit in the books on education written by the 'liberal philosophers' is the view that the state is a neutral, balancing mechanism that is above class conflict. Indeed, the existence of classes is rarely mentioned; society is pluralistic, consisting of numerous 'pressure' groups, the function of the state being merely to adjudicate amongst them in a neutral way.[5] The state itself is seen as a neutral instrument, mediating between particular competing interests in the 'national interest'. It is assumed that the state's main function is to make minor 'adjustments' so that the present system can operate more efficiently. Theories of democratic pluralism such as this are an expression of the bourgeois ideology of social democracy.

Against such democratic pluralist theories it could be argued that they are self-validating because they are based on two assumptions: that power is legitimate and that the state is neutral. They thus exclude by definition the possibility that the state's function might be to sustain and legitimize the power of a particular class. Second, these theories limit their criticism of the system to proposals for improving it through reform. Moreover, they cannot account for the substantial amount of counter-evidence.[6]

Schooling and capitalism

In contrast to the above bourgeois conception, a Marxist viewpoint argues that, as present constituted, education serves the interests of capital. I suppose one of the most influential accounts of education in the last few years from a Marxist position has been Bowles and Gintis's *Schooling in Capitalist America*.[7] Let me briefly outline their thesis.

Capitalist society is determined by the imperatives of profit and domination, but this formally totalitarian economic system is in contrast to the formally democratic political system. (This is why to make the hierarchical division of labour appear 'just' is not easy.) As most workers do not own the means of production, they have to sell their labour power. In the process of production workers produce not only material products but themselves as well. The economy produces people as well as commodities. One of several institutions which serve to perpetuate the structure of privilege is the family.

Like the educational system, the family plays a major role in preparing the young for economic and social roles. Families reproduce the forms of consciousness required for the integration of a new generation

47

into the economic system. Similarly, the educational system plays a central role in preparing individuals for the world of alienated and stratified work relationships. The reproduction of the social relations of production depends on the reproduction of consciousness. *How does schooling do this*?

First, it produces many of the technical and cognitive skills for adequate job-performance. The school produces and labels personal characteristics relevant to the staffing of positions in the hierarchy. It rewards certain capacities, whilst penalizing others. Schools produce personality traits and forms of consciousness which facilitate trouble-free integration into the existing hierarchic forms. Above all, workers must be dependable and diligent. There are also modes of self-presentation, such as manner of speech and dress, which take on a social-class character. The educational system, through the pattern of status distinctions it fosters, reinforces the stratified consciousness on which the fragmentation of subordinate classes is based. Schools at once supply labour to the dominant enterprises and reinforce the racial, ethnic, sexual and class segmentation of the labour force. It is argued that major aspects of educational organization *replicate* the relationships of dominance, and subordinancy in the economic sphere. There is a correspondence between the social relations of schooling and of work. This accounts for the ability of the educational system to produce an amenable and fragmented labour force.

Bowles and Gintis argue that employers have sought to use the schools for the reproduction of profitable types of worker consciousness, through a correspondence between the social relationships of education and those of economic life. Some streams (or tracks) emphasize rule-following and close supervision, while others emphasize internalization of norms. In this way the structure of social relations in education gets the student used to the discipline of the workplace, whilst developing certain modes of self-presentation. Working-class parents often seem to favour the stricter educational methods, which reflect their own work experiences, their submission to authority.

Working-class schools thus often have a type of social relationship that fairly closely mirrors that of the factory. There is this parallel in industry: successful job-performance at low hierarchical levels requires the workers' orientation towards rule-following and conformity to external authority. Successful performance at higher levels requires behaviour according to internalized norms. In other words, some schools seem to stress the future subordinate positions of its charges, and teach docility, whilst others stress the need for self-direction, the internalization of norms and the development of 'leadership'. These differential socialization patterns in schools, and within schools attended by students of different social classes, do not arise by accident. Personality traits conducive to performance at different hierarchical levels are fostered by the school system. That is to say, different levels of education feed workers into different levels within the occupational structure; in this way the social relations of education replicate the hierarchical division of labour. As Bowles and Gintis remark: 'The educational system works to justify economic unequality and to produce a labour force whose capacities, credentials, and consciousness are dictated in substantial measure by the requirements of profitable employment in the capitalist economy.'

Alienation and inequality have their roots not in human nature, not in technology, not in the educational system itself, but in the structure of the capitalist economy. Indeed, by integrating new generations into the social order, the schools are constrained to justify and reproduce inequality rather than correct it. The primary economic function of schooling, then, is not the production or selection of technical skills, but to facilitate the stratification of the labour force. The educational system legitimates economic inequality by providing an open and ostensibly meritocratic mechanism for assigning individuals to unequal economic positions. It is not geared for an egalitarian but an integrative function — towards the reproduction of economic relations. Education reproduces inequality by justifying privilege and attributing poverty to personal failure. But education, we are continually reminded, is not the source of the problem: 'the corporate capitalist economy — with its bias towards hierarchy, waste and alienation in production, and its mandate for a school system attuned to the reproduction and legitimation of the associated division of labour — may be seen as a source of the problem.'

In short, Bowles and Gintis believe that schools embody certain elements of industrial practice. The ranking of children in schools is replicated in the labour market, a process which represents the division between mental and manual labour.

Since their book was published in 1976 many criticisms of their thesis have emerged.[8] Their argument that there is a direct correspondence between relations of production in work and relations in school is, in many ways, over-simplistic. There are many schools where the practices contradict this thesis; there are numerous schools which are far more autonomous than they allow for. It has been said that their correspondence theory, which over-simplifies the education process, can lead to pessimism amongst teachers; if all that they are doing is directly reproducing pupils as units to be slotted into the labour market their job hardly seems worth doing. This is particularly the reaction of many student teachers on hearing such a thesis. I think that Bowles and Gintis would argue that the relationship of schools to the economy is not immediately visible to teachers, and that their aim was to demystify, to make explicit the social relations that were not readily admitted.

This point leads to another criticism: the Bowles and Gintis thesis focuses only on the form of education. They stress that the production process not only produces but reproduces the whole set of social constellations, the same type of people. For Gintis, the *content* of education is immaterial, it does not really matter what teachers teach their pupils. But many thoughtful teachers are very concerned about improving the curriculum. The Bowles and Gintis argument leads to a scepticism about the value of the work of those teachers who spend a lot of time and energy trying to make the curriculum more relevant.

It has also been pointed out that in Bowles and Gintis there is scarcely any reference to working-class culture, to the resistance and struggle of working-class politics. It is also said that in terms of strategy their book has little to offer, but I think this is an unrealistic expectation. On their behalf it could be argued that though individual schools do exist that do not meet the requirements of industry, nevertheless, the Bowles and Gintis thesis is correct on the level of the deeper structural patterns.

An important feature of the present situation is the growing reliance by industry on cultural forms and practices. In the nineteenth century, control of labour was direct but now industrialists are using social science to control labour. Gradually, the professions have become incorporated into capitalism. Psychology and sociology are now being used for profit maximization; industry is utilizing intellectual labour for the service of capital accumulation. Industrial psychology, like scientific management, are the new forms of social control. I mentioned earlier the increase in the service industries; with this shift there has been an increase in the (so-called 'caring') welfare professions. This may be leading to a more pervasive ideological/political control – but the effects of this absorption of intellectual labour by industry, the role of these new forms of cultural legitimation, are as yet uncertain.

It is agreed that, as Bowles and Gintis say, reproduction does take place – but not in the reductionist way that they argue. Reproduction takes place at different levels and in various forms. In short, education is much more heterogeneous than they realize.

Implicit in the work of Bowles and Gintis is the theory that the actions of the state flow more or less directly from the 'requirements of capital'. Capitalism develops according to certain laws of accumulation; there are mergers and takeovers until there exist a number of multinational corporations, giant monopolies. These make various demands on the state, which, in taking action to satisfy them, becomes increasingly drawn into production. Eventually the state is so involved that the state and capitalist corporations become virtually indistinguishable.

One of the problems with this view is that it is an economistic theory – it reduces the totality of capitalist social relations to those of the production process itself. The state apparatuses and institutions, like the educational system, are assumed to be simply functional to capital. According to Bowles and Gintis, education has no autonomy whatsoever. As their functionalist theory stresses function and reproduction, the notion of relative autonomy is neglected in their work; the articulations, the mediations, are missing, and this means that they cannot analyse questions such as the complex linkages between capital and state.

In the next section I return to the origins of the debate in the nineteenth century to focus on the radical view of education, the struggle of working-class people to create their own independent form (and content) of education. I do this in order to highlight what is, for me, one of the most important issues today: Is radical education possible at all within the state system and, if so, to what extent?

The radical view of education: bread, knowledge and freedom

I may have given the impression in previous sections that mass schooling was passively received by the working class, but this was not so. In recent years there has been a general recovery of early working-class radicalism, and Richard Johnson, who has done considerable work in the rediscovery of popular educational traditions, has suggested some of the salient features of radical education that should be explored.

Discussing working-class education in the early nineteenth century, Johnson notes that it was a tradition that was sharply oppositional.[9] There was a contestation of all orthodoxies; radicals critiqued all forms of 'education' whether provided by the church or state.

One of the main features was the development of alternative educational goals:[10]

At one level these embraced a vision of a whole alternative future...
At another, radicalism developed its own curricula and pedagogies,
its own definition of 'really useful knowledge' a characteristically
radical *content*, a sense of what it was really important to know.
Thirdly, radicalism conducted an important internal debate about
education as a political strategy or as a means of changing the world.
Like most aspects of counter-education, this debate was also
directed at dominant middle-class conceptions of the relations
between education and politics, especially the argument that

'national education' was a necessary condition for the granting of universal suffrage . . . Finally, radical movements developed a vigorous and varied education practice.

Radical education, then, was not just different in content from orthodox schooling, its *principles* were different. It attempted to break the distinction between 'education' and non-education (between school and everything outside school). Radicals made their own cultural inventions such as various kinds of reading and discussion groups, travelling lecturers, the use of newspapers as an educative medium. These formed a series of informal educational networks and exemplified their conception of knowledge – the view that education should be widely available and extensive in content. There was the conviction that real knowledge served practical ends for the knower, a concern that knowledge should be relevant to the problems experienced in life. And yet, despite this stress on the relation of knowledge to the knower's experience, it was not a narrow, pragmatic conception of knowledge.

The radical enthusiasm for education was composed of several strands, some of them in potential conflict. Although all radicals saw education as an aspect of equal rights and a goal to be fought for, education was also part of a political strategy. One of the interesting debates of the period, for example, concerned the question of social amelioration. Whilst some groups saw education as a sufficient remedy for social evils, others (like the followers of Robert Owen) argued that economic exploitation was so great that educational reform by itself was insufficient, and so it was important to secure political rights first. The Owenites wished to found their own schools, and to show the world how children really could be educated, but these projects invariably involved middle-class aid and loss of independence.

The Chartists were also involved in educational work, but their projects, too, became associated with middle-class philanthropy. When the political challenges were blunted and hopes of immediate success began to fail, different tactical and strategic questions emerged. Johnson relates that after the 1840s:[11]

> in the wake of the political defeats, independent working-class education continued . . . But it took on more individualistic forms ('self-education') or lost its connection with politics ('mutual improvement') or became the cultural preserve of the aristocracies. It certainly lost the ambition of being an alternative system . . . At the same time, a new kind of educational agitation began to emerge . . . Working-class activists began to demand education through the state.

The crucial point is this: during the beginning of the nineteenth century there existed various radical groups who believed that *an alternative working-class system of education was possible*. This strategy of substitution was followed till the 1850s and 1860s. It proved immensely difficult to carry out and was replaced by the demand for more equal access to facilities that were to be provided by the state. Johnson comments: [12]

> Thus while radicals, Chartists and Owenites all opposed state education except as the work of a transformed state, later socialists actually fuelled the growth of state schooling by their own agitations. The consequences of this adaptation were immense; it involved, for instance, accepting, in a very sharp form, the child-adult divide, the tendency to equate education with school, the depoliticization of educational content, and the professionalization of teaching. In all these ways the state as educator was by no means a neutral apparatus.

How can this shift be explained? Was it the effect of material improvements; the influence of the labour-aristocracy, bribed and corrupted, as Lenin said, in a thousand ways; or did it signify changes in the mode of hegemony or social control? Johnson suggests that the independent tradition of working-class education appears to have drawn on resources that could only have existed had capital's control of production and of the reproduction of labour power been relatively loose. That is to say, family households must have still possessed space or autonomy for educational activities. There then developed a more complete subordination of labour in production, and family/community autonomy was curtailed. [13] As indigenous educational resources were squeezed, education provided by the state was offered and enforced.

The rediscovery of popular educational traditions is important for several reasons. It makes people aware that the issues with which they are concerned are not new ones. In my own case, for example, it has given me an understanding of the struggle as an ongoing one, a recognition that there are partial defeats, that there are lessons to be learnt. It is important to realize that there did exist radical groups who fought for an alternative working-class system, but who lost the battle. [14] This strategy was replaced by the demand for more equal access to the facilities provided by the state but, as I suggested earlier, the 'equal opportunity' argument leads only to individual mobility and not to any radical changes in class structure.

Second, I have learnt that the split that is often perceived nowadays between 'alternative' and 'socialist' education did not exist at one time. The liberation threads (revived by Bertrand Russell, A.S. Neill and Paul Goodman from an anarchist tradition), are similar in content and aims to the autonomous socialist education movement; both rejected the state system as inevitably involving the incorporation of the working class. From the historical experience of these groups it is possible to learn of the dangers of incorporation, how the apparent growth of educational facilities, far from promising liberation, can bring about subjection. We can now begin to ask: Why is it that during this century with the rise of state education there has been a decline in the belief among the working class that knowledge is a weapon of liberation?

What is exemplary about Johnson's paper is that his analysis is not limited to the educational and political levels; in order to explain the shift in the strategies and forms of education, he concludes by giving a materialist analysis based on economic changes within capitalism itself, but at the same time he stresses that for nineteenth-century radical groups politics and education went together in a complex means-end relationship. Education without politics was thought inadequate; there was a recognition that education must be allied to an understanding of power. But politics without education was also found wanting. It is precisely this stress on education as an aspect of socialist politics that needs to be revived today.

Chapter 5

The increase in state intervention

The capitalist mode of production and its crises

Having looked at the origins of state education and the 'liberal' and 'Marxist' views of the relationship between education and the state, we must now try and understand the increasing intervention in education by the state during the last few years. In order to do this we need an understanding of *economic crises*, the contradictions within capital accumulation itself, which have led to the growth of state intervention.

The aim of capitalist production is to maximize profit. To acquire profits the capitalist must sell commodities at a lower price than that of his competitors. One of the most effective ways of doing this is to lower the production costs (the cost price) by increasing production. In the struggle to survive capitalists have to substitute ever more efficient and complex machines ('dead labour') for workers ('living labour'). Since the population and length of the working day cannot be expanded without limits, capital employs a greater proportion of machinery and raises labour productivity so that a greater amount of raw materials is worked on by a given amount of living labour.

The capital of all capitalists can be divided into two parts. The first part serves to buy machines, buildings and raw materials. Its value remains constant throughout production and it is therefore called *constant* capital. The second part is used to buy labour power, to pay wages, and is called *variable* capital. It is this part alone which produces surplus value. Marx called the dual relationship of constant and variable capital the organic composition of capital. And so the process of accumulation involves constant revolutions in the labour process and in the techniques of production. There is a scrapping of old techniques and the continual adoption of more productive ones. Now, if the organic composition of capital increases, the profit will tend to decline in relation to the total capital, because only variable capital produces surplus value. This is known as the law of the tendency of the rate of profit to fall (TRPF).

Let me try and make this process clearer: if you increase the productivity of labour you produce more commodities in the same time and so the value of each individual commodity falls. To have more value than before, a greater number of commodities have to be produced, which means that there has to be more capital investment. This process, however, is contradictory; although the productivity is increased, less labour is employed by a given amount of capital.

An increase in the productivity of labour, then, involves an increase in the organic composition of capital, more capital is invested as constant capital, on machinery and raw materials rather than variable capital (wages for labour power). It is crucial to remember that profits arise out of the exploitation of workers alone. As productivity increases there are relatively fewer workers exploited by a given amount of capital. This means that there is a tendency of the rate of profit to fall. The more capital is invested, the more the 'tendency of the rate of profit to fall' asserts itself. The state then intervenes to support the attempts of capital to push back the fall in the rate of profit, to postpone the consequences of the tendency.

State intervention

During the last fifteen years or so there has been a growth of the state's role in the capitalist economy. The state, more and more, has come to guarantee the conditions for private capital accumulation.[1] As David Yaffe has pointed out,[2]

State expenditure, by postponing the immediate consequences of the fall in the rate of profit, by allowing capital accumulation to expand, necessitates an increase of credit and therefore the money supply to finance its own expenditure. In such a way the State maintains the general conditions of capital accumulation, and supports the attempts of capital to stave off the fall in the rate of profit.

But state expenditure, by allowing the crisis to be postponed, exacerbates the very conditions that make state expenditure necessary, that is, the tendency of the rate of profit to fall.

Let us examine the effect of the increase of social services, health and education expenditure on the rate of profit of individual capital. The first point to note about state expenditure is that the capitalist state does not allow unemployment to increase beyond certain levels, and that unemployment benefits are a cost to capital, a deduction from surplus value. (Surplus value is the difference between the new value produced by labour in the process of production and the cost of reproducing labour power. In a capitalist society surplus value is produced by wage labourers, and represents labour not paid for but appropriated by the capitalist class.) Education seems to have largely an ideological function as only a very small amount of education is useful for capitalist production in the sense of increasing surplus value.

The growth of the education sector is a deduction from the mass of profits of the capitalist class. The same is true of health, except that there are no ways in which health can offset the cost involved. The financing of the state sector (education, health, police, administration), is a deduction from an already insufficient mass of profits, in relation to the total amount of capital which has been invested.

Most education does not contribute to increasing the value of labour power. Educational expenditure, as a whole, does not contribute to the increase of profits. That is why in an economic crisis expenditure is cut back and a shift of emphasis takes place towards the more 'technical' aspects of schooling. The teachers who are engaged in training productive workers are involved with changing the commodity labour-power itself. But it should be remembered that if labour power with a particular skill becomes too expensive the capitalist can introduce another method of production which does not need that skill.[3]

Most workers in capitalist society today are unproductive; they are a majority now, and this means that most education is going on unproductive workers anyway. Marx's distinction between productive and unproductive labour is this: if labour directly increases the mass of surplus value it is productive, if it does not produce surplus value it is unproductive. Many state and commercial workers are classified as unproductive because they do not produce surplus value; these workers, paid not by capital but out of revenue, are becoming increasingly significant in modern capitalism. An important point about state employees is that their labour is not directly under the control of capital and is not directly subject to the coercive force of competition. One of the reasons why the distinction between productive and unproductive labour is crucial is that in times of crises the capitalist state cuts expenditure in those areas where many unproductive workers are employed, in health and welfare services, *and education*. This is because they involve unproductive expenditure, their financing reduces the proportion of surplus value which is available for accumulation as capital. Cuts in education, welfare services, etc., therefore, redistribute surplus value from unproductive expenditure to capital.

The state sector is financed either out of taxation or through deficit financing (future taxation). In a sense, taxation can be seen as a deduction from the profits of the capitalist class. However, 'wage freezes' and 'social contracts' are attempts to make sure that, as inflation increases, more and more of the growth of taxation falls on the working class and is actually a deduction from working-class wages.

To sum up; the growth of the state is a necessary condition for allowing capital accumulation to proceed, but, nevertheless, the fact that a large share of the growing surplus value has to go to the state means that the rate of profit falls faster than would otherwise be the case for the individual capitalist. It was mentioned earlier that as productivity increases, fewer and fewer workers are employed by a given amount of capital. The growth of state expenditure and the maintenance of 'full' employment exacerbates this process. To resolve the crisis, to re-establish the conditions for a higher rate of profit, one strategy is to increase unemployment massively, and to reduce wages below the value of labour power – but this contradicts the 'welfare' policies of the capitalist state.

Though Marx put forward as a law of capitalism that the rate of profit has a tendency to fall, it should be emphasized that when Marx refers to an economic law he explicitly means a tendency. He pointed out that there are also *counter-balancing forces* such as the increasing intensity of exploitation, depression of wages, the cheapening of the elements of constant, and variable capital. The tendency and counteracting tendencies exist in a contradictory unity. Another way of putting this is that the disease is also a form of the cure; the least efficient capitalist firms become bankrupt and only the more productive capitals survive. A move towards the greater concentration and centralization of capitals takes place. In the present conjuncture, then, we are witnessing an attack on state expenditure – an attempt to restructure capital to a greater profitability. The restructuring of capital can temporarily resolve the contradictions which give rise to crises. The processes by which the crisis counteracts the falling rate of profit may sometimes restore the conditions for accumulation, but in overcoming the contradiction, the barrier to accumulation, the crisis removes it to a higher level. The proletariat is forced to struggle against the expulsion of living labour and the restructuring of capital. This struggle is determined by the antagonistic relation of capital and labour. It is only in this context that we can understand the problems of schooling and the state.

One of the reasons for the recent controversies in this area is that there are many differing theories of the state. These differ partly because of the social location of the theorists concerned, the historical developments that have taken place, and the changes in the role of the state itself. But not only is the state constantly changing, people's conceptions of it are also changing. The rest of the chapter is a discussion of some contemporary conceptualizations of the state.

Some conceptions of the state

The neutral state: social democracy, education and reform

The first feature to be noted is the strength and pervasiveness of social democratic ideology in Britain. This ideology is a very important component of the social formation because of its links with both capital and the state. The most effective agent of social democratic ideology and practice is the Labour Party.

The British Labour Party has always had a problematic relationship with capital; the party's main characteristics are, first, its lack of contact with Marxist thought, and, second, its entrenched belief in social democracy – the view that parliamentarism can bring about socialism through reform of a capitalist society.[4] Labourism, then, is associated with social democratic ideology which has a long tradition in the British social formation and permeates all levels, the economic, political, social and educational. One of its main features is that it propagates the notion that the state is neutral. In this view, as the state is above class, somewhat like an independent adjudicator, it can be democratically lobbied in the interest of the working class.

For a period after the Second World War social democratic ideology focused on educational *reform*. The 'failure' of working-class children had been pointed out by many sociologists of education and Fabian (Labour Party) intellectuals. It was argued that working-class failure was brought about by a lack of opportunity. It was assumed that if working-class children were given the opportunity to be educationally 'successful', society would, somehow, become egalitarian. The problem was narrowly conceived of as being one merely of 'access' rather than of class domination. In social democratic ideology it is taken for granted that the 'imperfections' of society can be gradually modified and that 'cultural deprivation' and 'disadvantage' can be overcome by such reforms. As the state is neutral – perhaps even a benevolent institution which can act to compensate the underprivileged – the task of social policy is to persuade government to take legal measures which make possible equal access to education.

Education in post-war Britain was largely shaped by an alliance between the Labour Party, a specialized group of intellectuals from the (relatively new) discipline of sociology of education, and the teachers' unions.[5] This alliance, holding a social democratic ideology, had a particular conception of education. Education was an investment both for the individual and society. The aim of this dual investment was the production of people who were both capable industrial workers and participants in 'democracy'. It was stressed that individuals should realize their potentialities but the emphasis was always on the individual, not the class. It was generally held, for example, that intellectual capacities were based on crucial innate differences.

From the social democratic viewpoint, reform, then, is always seen in terms of access to education, of 'equal opportunity'. Questions regarding the content and control of education are not subjects for discussion. Thus the formulation of the problem already defines that the solution will be within acceptable parameters. The solutions of social democracy are always based on an evolutionary view of change and are unapologetically reformist.

It is through the establishment of bourgeois social democracy that political parties based on working-class support have become part of the state apparatus. This enables the working class to have the appearance of political power, and maintains the illusion that the state is neutral. The reason I am emphasizing social democratic ideology and practice, and the Labour Party as its main agent, is that it is this historical alliance which has effectively 'contained' the contradictions of capitalist society; it always *defuses* class conflict and allows capital to reproduce itself.

Though I reject the pervasive social democratic view that the state is neutral, I want to mention here a similar debate that is occurring about 'the rule of law'. Is the law above class, is it neutral? There is considerable controversy on the Left about what is meant by the 'rule of law'. Some social theorists, like E.P. Thompson, contend that the law is not a mirage, a cover for class rule. In a social democracy, whatever the distortions, the law is above class, it is basically neutral. This means that the law is not merely an instrument in the hands of the ruling class to exercise power, but also one to limit it.

Thompson argues that there is a difference between arbitrary power and the rule of law. He feels that we ought to expose the shams and inequities which may be concealed beneath this law, but the rule of law itself, the imposing of effective inhibitions upon power and the defence of the citizen from power's all-intrusive claims, seems to him to be an unequalled human good. He insists that the rule of law has not only been imposed upon people from above; it has also been a medium within which other social conflicts have been fought out. The law, as a logic of equity, must always seek to transcend the inequalities of class:[6]

> We reach, then, not a simple conclusion (law = class power) but a complex and contradictory one. On the one hand, it is true that the law did mediate existent class relations to the advantage of the rulers. On the other hand, the law mediated these class relations through legal forms, which imposed, again and again, inhibitions

upon the actions of the rulers . . . And not only were the rulers (indeed, the ruling class as a whole) inhibited by their own rules of law against the exercise of direct unmediated force, but they also believed enough in these rules, and in their accompanying ideological rhetoric, to allow, in certain areas, the law itself to be a genuine forum within which certain kinds of class conflict were fought out.

In opposition to this is the view of Pashukanis, who asserts that the law is embedded in social relations in a material way.[7] The law establishes a framework which assures the 'rights of the individual', bourgeois property rights. The law sets the parameters within which capital accumulation — and all that it implies — can be assured. This view contends that the law is inherently bourgeois; it is functional for capitalism. Under socialism it will be liquidated; there will be a historical transcendence of the legal form.

One of the weaknesses of the Left, as the above polemic shows, is that it has failed to adequately theorize the rule of law. The law is often presented as if it was some Kantian ideal, or a hegemonic ideology. It is neither a neutral instrument nor is it above class. The law is heterogeneous and contradictory, an arena of class struggle. As it changes over time, we must study it historically and ask: where does the law come from? Why does social control in certain historical periods take the form of *legal* control? At the moment we lack a systematic approach to the relations *between* the different institutions of *social control*. What is the precise relationship, for example, between the law, political parties and the media; between the law and the family, racial policies and education?

Now, according to some observers, there is a move towards the corporate state. In corporativism, the state, which is now playing a much stronger role, combines with both capital and labour; there is a growing interdependence between the Confederation of British Industry and the trade unions, and an integration of these organizations into economic planning. It is held that because of the increasing monopolization of capital, more planning of a long-term nature is required. Corporativism can be seen as a strategy for incorporating the working class by involving it in long-term planning. (But, of course, it should be remembered that the concentration of capital also aids the concentration of the proletariat, that is to say, the collectivization of labour.) There is an increase in centralized collective bargaining (pay, price, and investment policies) at the level of the state, which acts as a legitimizing force. This tendency thus stresses a harmonist view, that of class collaboration. And so, in the mass media there are discussions of the need for 'participation', the development of 'community relations', and of 'democracy'.

The Labour Party's attempt to focus public attention on education (through initiating the 'Great Debate' in 1976) may well have been a tactical device to shift attention away from insuperable economic problems. But it was more than this — it marked a shift in policy. It should be remembered that it was under the aegis of a social democratic party that there was an attack on progressive education (Chapter 1); a shift towards the enforcement of stricter discipline (Chapter 2); and the attempt to gear schooling more tightly with the 'needs' of industry (Chapter 3). As I have shown, a great deal of discussion has taken place recently about the origins, development and use of 'discipline'. The repressive apparatus has gained strength in recent years. There has been a movement towards what is called 'the strong state'.

Towards the strong state

As the crisis has deepened, there has been a change in the modalities of control, a major shift towards coercion by the interventionist capitalist state. But one has to explain this shift, the reason why it has taken this particular form in the present historical conjuncture. As I mentioned in Chapter 3, Gramsci's discussion of hegemony is helpful in an understanding of the drift towards the routine use of the more repressive features of the state. Hegemony, for Gramsci, refers not only to the economic and political control exercised by the dominant class, but also to its success in projecting its own particular way of seeing life and the world, so that this is accepted as 'common sense' and part of the natural order by those who are in fact subordinated to it. Hegemony, then, involves the dialectical relation of class forces, the organization of consent, which has to be fought for on the terrain of civil society.[8] Unlike Althusser, Gramsci does not rigidly demarcate some state apparatus as having an ideological function and others as having a repressive function. Gramsci suggests that each apparatus has both; coercion and consent are always present, but the question is: which aspect has dominance at a certain period? The law is one such apparatus. The legal and juridical formation consisting of institutional practices seems to be full of contradictions, such as the co-existence of both consensual and coercive aspects.

A book by Stuart Hall *et al.*, called *Policing the Crisis*, focuses on these themes — it shows how a consensus was developed in Britain for the more coercive apparatuses to have increased dominance.[9] The authors begin by considering how mugging became a black crime, how 'mugging' came to equal 'blacks'. The researchers found that, at the level of structures, there is a symbiotic relationship between the police, the judiciary and the media. Apparently the police were active before the press utilized the term 'mugging'. In 1972 some youths received very heavy sentences and a social reaction occurred that was out of all proportion with the events: 'a moral panic'. The media, which had first focused on permissiveness, turned to questions of law and violence. The press said that mugging was a new crime when in fact it was a new label (from the United States) for an old one. Mugging was described in emotive terms such as 'violent lawlessness'; the word seemed to conjure up visions of the complete disintegration of society. The ground was being prepared.

The authors convincingly demonstrate how many members of the bourgeoisie experienced a crisis of authoriy in the 1960s. They felt their values to be threatened and thought that their traditional ways of living were being lost. There was social anxiety, for example, about the sale of drugs, the rising crime rate, the spread of pornography and permissiveness, the threat to the British way of life by black immigrants.

Stuart Hall, utilizing a thesis of Antonio Gramsci, has suggested that the state has a hegemonic function and that all its apparatuses have coercive and consensual aspects. Both these aspects are always present but there are shifts between them, different aspects having dominance at various times. What happened, in Britain, was that a concern developed about law and order. There was a 'debate' about it in the press, and a succession of 'moral panics' was created by working on people's genuine anxieties. In other words, the media used 'popular ventriloquism' to structure the debate. There was a call to maintain cultural and educational standards, to preserve traditional values. Thus a popular discourse developed around the question of law and order. It appeared as if there was an appeal from below for action by a strong state. In this way a popular demand was constructed; there seemed to be a popular consent for the use of authority and stricter discipline. This type of mobilization is a new way of creating consent.

Related to this process — the development of a populist consent for coercion — is the revival of the political Right in Britain over the last few years, and the development of a new type of conservatism. The political Right has been very successful in utilizing the field of popular practice, and mobilizing opinion towards an authoritarian populism which justifies, legitimizes, the strong directive state. In practical terms this has meant that the social and political agenda has been set by the political Right. It has effectively condensed a wide range of social and political issues and themes such as permissiveness, law and order, strikes, social security abuse, and immigration. The development of 'the strong state', to a large extent, is an anticipation of sharpening industrial and political struggle. As the crisis deepens,[10]

the anxieties of the lay public and the perceived threats to the State coincide and converge. The State comes to provide a 'sense of direction' which the lay public feels, society has lost . . . The State can now, publicly and legitimately, campaign against the 'extremes' on behalf and in defence of the majority. [And so] the power of the State is directed against the organized power of the working class; against political extremism; against trade union blackmail; against the threat of anarchy, riot and terrorism.

This shift towards coercion by the state can be clearly seen in the area of race relations. Under the guise of a concern with public order an attempt is being made to discipline blacks. There is increased surveillance; black youths are arrested on suspicion and daily face police harassment and intimidation. Young black people, most severely hit by the current crisis, have few options open to them. Racism is becoming a popular ideology and even 'moderates' now accept racist laws and policies. It must be emphasized that ideologies are not some sort of 'false consciousness' but are based on actual lived relations. I shall explore these problems more deeply when I discuss (in Chapter 8) the themes of race, imperialism and education.

In education, the move towards stricter discipline is related to the increasing centralization and concentration of power. This can be seen at the level of government policy; it is apparent in the reorganization of the Inspectorate, for example, its increasing control of the curriculum, its monitoring and assessment of pupil performances. But the objection could be made that a concentration of power is not really taking place; there is, in fact, a movement towards decentralization, the granting of more autonomy at local level. I concede this and suggest that the trend may serve several purposes. First, it has an ideological function, it can be said that decentralization aids representative/ participatory democracy. But such a policy of decentralized, that is to say, fragmented organizations can also provide an effective obstacle to those seeking social change. (Consider, for example, how many local education authorities prevented the setting up of genuine comprehensive schools.) Moreover, it has been realized that a decentralized system is safer because it is more difficult to subvert. For example, a central computer system is so vulnerable that policies of dispersion are now being adopted. For these reasons, I would suggest that there is a contradictory trend; on one level there is an increasing centralization of education in terms of power, but there are also, at other levels, lesser tendencies towards decentralization.

In this and previous chapters I have attempted to set some of the recent developments in the sociology of education within the context of the crisis of capitalism, to provide the basis for an understanding of the present conjuncture. A conjuncture consists not just of one period of time, but can contain many periods with many contradictions within them. According to Althusser, a conjuncture is the central concept of the Marxist science of politics; it denotes the exact balance of forces, the state of overdetermination of the contradictions at any given moment, to which political tactics must be applied. I would argue that in the present conjuncture an important role is being played in the British social formation by the representative, interventionist state. It is *'representative'* in the sense that the state has instituted universal suffrage and a working parliamentary system. This allows the state to emphasize consent to its authority, thus legitimizing it. The *interventionist* aspect of the state is exemplified in its management of demand. The state, in short, secures certain conditions of existence of capitalism.

The intervention of the bourgeois state arises directly from the needs of capital. Capital requires certain general conditions which it is unable to guarantee as many, individual, capitals. The state, in its capacity as guarantor of the conditions of capital accumulation, has to ensure the maintenance of the basic production industries. The demands put upon labour power by capital have resulted in the intervention of the state in the reproduction of labour power itself. Besides health, education is, of course, the main sector concerned with the reproduction of labour power.

Several recent developments in state relations have been stressed in this chapter. First, the increasing use of legal and juridical forms for the purpose of control by the state; second, the marked tendency, in certain periods, towards 'collaboration' between unions and the state. This can be seen in the formulation of jointly agreed policies (or an agreement about basic presuppositions such as reformist politics). Third, the most salient fact: the growing nexus between state and capital. One of the main contradictions for the state during this period is that whilst attempting to retain its representative aspect through bourgeois hegemony, it has to justify and legitimize its increasingly interventionist role in the long-term interests of capital.

Chapter 6

The growing nexus between state and capital

Introduction

In this chapter I shall outline how the capitalist mode of production can be periodized into three stages: *laissez-faire*, monopoly, and state monopoly capitalism. It will be argued that the distinguishing feature of state monopoly capitalism is the state's predominance in economic reproduction. I shall raise the questions: How far does the state directly serve the interests of capital? What is the precise nature of the articulation between capital and state? Why is the state, in late capitalism, playing such an increasingly interventionist role? These issues are discussed in a section which outlines some of the recent Marxist debates on the state. Is the state in capitalist society, or is it a capitalist state? I focus on the theories of Miliband and of Poulantzas, and then on the work of Holloway and Picciotto. I go on to show how deepening crises lead to increasing unemployment. The state directly intervenes and there is a growth of state expenditure. The state attempts to restructure capital – but it can only exacerbate the crisis. In the final section I draw a parallel between the tensions that exist in the nationalized industries and in education. At a time of crisis the character of both institutions begins to change. New criteria begin to be enforced. It is suggested that these changes must be seen as a part of a process of struggle over the restructuring of social relations in education.

Capitalism and the state

Marx showed that when there is a change in the mode of production there is a change in the possession and control of means of production exercised by producing and non-producing classes. He argued that the feudal mode of production passes through various stages in its movement to capitalism. The differing forms of appropriation are accompanied by differing institutional forms of control. This creates new objects of class struggle. Following Marx, Ben Fine and Lawrence Harris have identified three stages in their periodization of the capitalist mode of production; *laissez-faire*, monopoly, and state monopoly capitalism.[1] It is accumulation under capitalist relations, and the class struggle associated with it, that are the basic forces determining the transformation of the capitalist mode from one stage to another.

In *laissez-faire* capitalism the production of surplus value increasingly came to rely upon the lengthening of the working day. During this stage, working-class militancy is expressed in the form of riots. There is a lack of working-class representation, and the state restricts reforms rather than grants them. In the transition from *laissez-faire* to monopoly capitalism, the latter gradually wrests political and economic control from parochial capital. There also occurs a transformation of state power.

Under *monopoly capitalism* machinery is used to replace living labour, and so there is an expulsion and deskilling of labour. There is a centralization of capital and, corresponding to the new forms of control at this stage, there exist new forms of appropriation of surplus value. During this period there is an intensification of class struggles over economic crises. The labour aristocracy acts to limit working-class action, to moderate economic struggle, to channel it towards social reformism.[2] There are many contradictory tendencies under monopoly capitalism that both promote and moderate class struggle. This can be seen in the development of the economic role of the state.

The distinguishing feature of *state monopoly capitalism*, it could be said, is the state's predominance in economic reproduction. In earlier stages the main social mechanisms for controlling production were the coercive forces of market exchange and the credit system; at this stage 'state intervention' is the pre-eminent mechanism. The state replaces the private credit system as the dominant agency through which capitalist accumulation is regulated.

Having made some brief remarks on the periodization of capitalism, it is time for me to take a closer look at the state. In the last few years there has been, besides the renaissance of Marxist political economy, a renewal of the debate on the state. It has to be admitted that, at the moment, Marxist theories of the state are still only tentative and fragmentary. One reason is that both state and capital are continually changing, and it is not possible to 'read off' developments within the state from the interests of capitalism in any simple way. And so we need to develop a deeper theoretical understanding of the state, and the relationship between state and capital. But this does not mean that the discussion is an academic one. The recent interest in the theories of the state has a political impetus, a concern to develop strategies in a wide range of economic, political and cultural struggles. The main problems are these: How should the state be conceptualized? What is the linkage between state and capitalism? In the last chapter we began to consider these questions; we now turn to a detailed consideration of them.

There are two common views of the state. First, there is the theory that the state has a dynamic of its own; this can be called the 'state in capitalist society' view. Second, there is the theory that the state is organized by capitalism: the 'capitalist state' view. One of the major debates concerns this question: is the state in capitalism or is it a capitalist state?

First, the 'state in capitalism' view; if it is theorized that the state (though related to) is separate from capitalism, and if it is seen as acting, at present, in the economic interests of the bourgeoisie, then it is also conceivable that the state could act in the interests of the working class. But this theory is based on the assumption that the state is neutral and that it can be merely taken over as it is, and made to act on behalf of the working class.

Against 'the state in capitalism' view, there are theorists who hold 'the capitalist state' view and argue that the state is 'shot through' in all its institutions, activities, functions, with the dictates of capitalism. The state is not neutral and separate, but is permeated with capitalist imperatives. Let us now examine these two approaches in more detail.

The 'state in capitalism' view

I shall begin with a brief outline of Poulantzas's theory of the state. Perhaps the best way of understanding his view is to describe the theory to which he is opposed. Poulantzas's work is a reaction against those humanist theories that stress that state policy is being determined by particular personnel. Miliband, for example, who argues like this, claims to show that the state is controlled by the capitalist class. Not only do many members of this class occupy powerful positions within the state (or have social links, common backgrounds, shared values with those who do), but some of them also control institutions such as the law, mass media or universities.[3] That is to say, there is an instrumental exercise of power by members of the capitalist class in strategic positions either directly through the formulation of state policy, or indirectly through concerted pressure on the state.

In contrast, Poulantzas's structuralist theory sees state policy as being determined by the necessity to reproduce capitalist social relations in general. He shifts the emphasis from particular personnel, who occupy positions of state power — to the structural requirements of capital.[4] In his view, capital is faced with two problems: first, there is the anarchy of the system; second, there is the potential solidarity of the working class. The state, therefore, has to act as an agency of cohesion *and* as an agency of fragmentation. Since the state is relatively autonomous, it can impose unity on competing capitals and, at the same time, its actions in fragmenting the potential solidarity of the working class can be seen as legitimate. In short, state institutions and activities are seen as serving the function of maintaining the structural requirements for the survival of the capitalist mode of production.

Poulantzas argues that the bourgeoisie as a political force is not a unity which then acts through the state; instead its unity is itself formed through the state. A concrete example of this point, the state acting as a unifying force for the bourgeoisie, may be helpful. Marx showed, in the case of Factory Acts, that intervention in the interests of capital as a whole was necessarily undertaken by the state. This was because economic competition prevented the bourgeoisie as a class from adopting the Acts because if any one capitalist introduced shorter hours he would be defeated in competition by the others. It is competition in particular circumstances, then, which forces the state to act in the interest of the bourgeoisie as a whole against the immediate interests of some of its fractions.

Poulantzas has been criticized for trying to develop an abstract theory about the general nature of the capitalist state, a theory which abstracts from the existence of national states. Moreover, it is said that there is no clarification of the specific mechanisms by which the interests of capital in general and those of the individual capitalists are articulated.[5]

Now, despite important differences, both Miliband and Poulantzas conceive of the state as a distinct entity (directly or indirectly serving the interests of capital). Both theorists analyse the state, implicitly or explicitly, as external to the dynamics of the capitalist mode of production. In seeing the state as a set of independent institutions or agencies, they reproduce that separation of the economic and political which is characteristic of bourgeois sociology, economics, and political theory. To put it in another way, it is a mistake to think of the state as being concerned only with political relations or to identify it with the political level. As Poulantzas stresses the relative autonomy of political relations, he underestimates the role played by the state in economic reproduction. The capitalist state exists to guarantee the reproduction of the social *and* economic relations of capital. That is to say, the state is a focus for class relations at political, economic and ideological levels and its institutions intervene in class struggle at all these levels.

The 'capitalist state' view

Though there are many different theories within the 'capitalist state' view, I will focus on the influential capital-relation school which is represented in Britain by the work of John Holloway and Sol Picciotto.[6] They argue against both Miliband and Poultanzas because of their way of separating the political from the economic. Second, they insist that Miliband and Poulantzas are incorrect to analyse the state as a 'thing', a separate entity in capitalist society. Structuralist theories of the state, in particular, are severely criticized by Holloway and Picciotto. They object to Poulantzas's theory because it is not developed from a concept of capital; it is said that he draws a distinction between the political and economic levels (or instances) and *separates* them, he focuses on the political and takes the economic level for granted.

Holloway and Picciotto believe that the contradictions of accumulation have too often been thought of as 'economic laws' operating from the outside upon political class relations. The state has been thought of as 'the state in capitalist society' rather than as being itself one aspect of the social relations of capital. In the 'capitalist state' view (which Holloway and Picciotto support) the state is part and parcel of capitalist social relations. And so the present crisis is not merely an 'economic crisis', but a crisis of the capital relation; it involves the totality of capitalist social relations.

It is worth outlining the Holloway-Picciotto argument in detail. Their starting point is a critique of economism *and* politicism. Economism is the view that the 'base' determines the 'superstructure', that the state and its institutions directly reflect the stage and characteristics of the economic base. Politicism is the view that the state has autonomy from the economic base. Both economism and politicism are criticized as being reductionist. The beginnings of a theory of the state must lie neither in the specificity of the political nor in the dominance of the economic, but in the historical materialist category of the capital relation.

Marx's project in *Capital* was to demonstrate that what appear as things in capitalism (e.g. prices, wages, etc.) are in fact shot through with the social relations of capitalism. Similarly, Holloway and Picciotto understand the state as not being a 'thing' but a 'form of the capital relation'. Using the concept 'state form', they argue that the state is not a thing which has a material existence; the state has meaning only as a form which interpenetrates all communal institutions. The state is itself one aspect of the social relations of capital and therefore stamped throughout its ideology, in all its institutions and procedures, with the contradictions of capital.

It is important to note that in bourgeois ideology there is a separation of the state from production. Within the capitalist mode of production wage labour and capital are supposed to come 'freely' to the market place. Whilst in feudal and slave societies coercion was an integral aspect of economic relations, with capitalism there is a separation of the means of coercion and the point of production. The worker is separated into worker and citizen. This separation into forms determined by capital, the separation of the economic and the political as two forms of class domination, gives rise to illusions about the autonomy of 'the state' from 'the economy'. The state, like other social forms in capitalism, is seen as a thing that stands apart from other things. Seen through the prism of the state, the capital relation is concealed; classes are atomized into a mass of individual citizens ('the public'), and the class struggle is defused.

Let me try and make the Holloway-Picciotto position clearer. They argue that whatever the function of a state institution, whether it is the law-courts, the police, the army, or the school, it sets out to establish and re-establish the capital relation. (I take 'the capital relation' to mean class domination in capitalist society.) They then remark that attempts to employ new technologies in order to increase relative surplus value entail the expulsion of living labour to the ranks of the unemployed. This expulsion is, at the same time, the expulsion of the only element in production that can produce surplus value. As a consequence there is a tendency in capitalism for the rate of profit to fall. But in order to offset this process the state attempts to mobilize counter-tendencies. These counter-tendencies operate at all levels, and are an attempt to restructure capital relations.

In contrast to the politicist theories of Miliband and Poulantzas, which I outlined earlier, Holloway and Picciotto emphasize the unity between political and economic reproduction. They insist that under capitalism the structure of social relations creates the illusion of a separation between economic and political struggles and that there is a strong tendency for struggles to be confined to economistic issues. In their view, the working class is mistakenly confined to economic struggle and fails to see that in reality economic and political relations are parts of a unity. They therefore make an appeal for a unification of political and economic struggles.

Whilst some versions of the 'capitalist state' theory are excessively abstract and neglect the importance of class struggle (thus reducing history to 'the logic of capital'), Holloway and Picciotto attempt to overcome these limitations by focusing on struggle, both between competing capitals and between capital and labour, in order to understand the present crisis and the role of the state. They argue that the crisis is not merely an economic one, but a crisis of accumulation which involves the *totality* of capitalist social relations.

Though I largely accept the Holloway and Picciotto view of the state and find it most helpful in many ways, particularly their wish to stress the unity of social relations, I do have some reservations. I believe that their analysis of the relationship between politics and economics is based on a limited conception of the main economic categories of Marx. The Holloway-Picciotto position does not sufficiently emphasize Marx's value theory and, in particular, the significance of the law of the tendency of profit to fall – a tendency which arises from the contradictions within capitalism itself.

The view that I have emphasized in this book is that state monopoly capitalism is a stage when the state directly participates or intervenes in the economy – it is a stage in which the law of concentration and centralization of capital remains valid; a stage in which crises exist and the law of the tendency of the rate of profit to fall and its counteracting influences operate. As long as capital remains, the technical composition has a tendency to rise, and this produces the tendency of the rate of profit to fall and its counteracting influences. These processes are the basis of capitalist crises. The state then directly intervenes in the restructuring of productive capital through its position as an agent controlling the economy at all levels.

The tendency for the rate of profit to fall gives rise to a tendency for crises and increases in unemployment. Now, the state is committed to expenditure in order to maintain a certain 'acceptable' level of employment. But in doing so it produces a further contradiction: the growth of state expenditure itself intensifies the tendency of the rate of profit to fall. This occurs because state expenditure must be financed by the taxation of surplus value produced by capital, since state expenditure (except for nationalized industries) does not itself produce surplus value. In other words, the state, in attempting to overcome crises, merely intensifies the source of crises and assures their inevitability.

Whilst my own position tends to place its emphasis on the economic origins of the crisis, the inherent contradictions within capitalism itself, for Holloway and Picciotto the crisis is neither economic nor political, it is a crisis of the capital relation. Crises are the effect of failure to maintain the domination of capital over labour, rather than the result of the logic of capitalism. A crisis inevitably involves a restructuring of the capital relation, which necessarily takes economic, political and ideological forms. In the next section we will focus on the restructuring of one state apparatus: education.

The restructuring of state education

I want to refer briefly to some of the contradictions within nationalized industries, to draw some parallels and stress the point that there are similar tensions and problems in education. Some years ago the British state was forced to ensure an orderly restructuring through nationalization. The state moderated and transformed the demands for workers' control; and yet at the same time its economic intervention was not subject to the direct control by financial criteria. That the nationalized industries are a site for struggle can be seen by the fact that on the one hand it is in the interest of capital to struggle for employment to be operated productively, that is to say, for the production of surplus value. On the other hand, working-class interest requires the operation of state employment unproductively for capital, the planned production of use values and the maintenance of employment.

Nationalization thus involves an ever-present tension between the interests of the working class, which requires it as a step towards proletarian control of the economy, and those of the bourgeoisie which requires its operation as capital. It can be noticed that in crises the character of nationalized industries starts to change. They begin to conform more closely to their operation as capital; the expulsion of living labour is forced forward as criteria of commercial profitability are enforced.

Similarly, the educational system is a site of struggle, exemplifying the tension between those who wish to transform it as a part of a revolutionary process and those for whom the school is largely an agency of social reproduction and control. Let me put this in another way: there is the struggle of the working class to secure opportunities and benefits for itself through education, but underlying this there is also the continuing struggle by capital to ensure the reproduction of the necessary social relations.

Just as the character of nationalized industries begins to change during a crisis, so do schools. Indeed, this book began with a description of some of the recent events and tendencies in schools and I said that they were related to a crisis. We went deeper, analysed the cause of the present economic crisis, and then discussed different conceptualizations of the state, and the relation between state and capital. The manifestations of the crisis, discussed in the early chapters, can now be seen as what they really are: attempts at a restructuring of the capital relation. It has been argued that current changes must be seen as a process of struggle over the restructuring of social relations. Capital is attempting to re-establish its dominance. Let me now recapitulate some of the ways in which capital is attempting to impose its domination over education.

For capital, schools contain several potential dangers: first, the teachers themselves may not act according to traditional, bourgeois norms and values. Consciously or unconsciously, teachers may be undermining the expectation that pupils should be willing, co-operative (submissive?) individuals. There is a fear of a breakdown in the control of teachers. After all, though teachers are employees of the state, how are these agents to be controlled to ensure that they reproduce the necessary bourgeois relations? And so it is said that they have too much autonomy. They must be made 'accountable'. This fear was a contributory factor in the attack from the Right on progressive teachers, their view of knowledge, methods, and their model of the pupil as an active, questioning and critical learner. This was one of the main themes of Chapter 1.

In the educational system of the 1960s, teachers appeared to have some autonomy and were allowed to experiment with progressive teaching methods. It could be argued that this approach was directed at creating an adaptable, flexible, labour force. In the 1980s, however, the situation is very different. Now it is asserted that progressive education, with its emphasis on personal development and autonomy, creates a social environment which diverges too much from most work situations. At a time of increasing international competition (and when developments in the labour process and the use of the new technology have reduced the scope for individual initiative) capital needs socialized workers willing to produce commodities in conformity with defined standards within fixed time-limits. The attack on progressive education, then, should be seen as part of *the ideological restructuring of the content and organization of schooling*.

But what does 'restructuring' entail? If the crisis is a crisis in the social relationship of domination and consent, restructuring represents an attempt by capital to use the state apparatus to reassert its control. It is restructuring, and not merely 'cutting', because the reassertion of control and maintenance involves the expansion of public expenditure in certain areas rather than a reduction. I am referring, for example, to the increase in the repressive state apparatuses such as the army and police. But within the education system, too, there is an increase in expenditure in certain areas (such as careers guidance, disruptive units, research into assessment, the core-curriculum). It should be noted that restructuring takes place not only at the economic level, but at the political and ideological levels as well.

Another prevalent fear is that pupils and students themselves may not accept the imposition of capital relations. Again, there is the anxiety that the breakdown in the control of young people has reached unacceptable proportions. This feeling legitimizes the enforcement of stricter discipline. It was suggested that the fear about the failure to control pupils is being expressed in the anxiety about 'educational standards' and moral values, the growth of truancy and indiscipline. I mentioned, for example, the rapid spread of disruptive units for children deemed 'trouble-makers' at school. And so the demand is that schools conform more closely in their operation to disciplinary institutions – the main topic of Chapter 2.

The theme of submission to the discipline of capitalist society was continued in Chapter 3 on work-socialization. At the same time as institutions become more disciplinary, the criteria of commercial and industrial relevance are increasingly enforced. It was stated that the point of various training schemes is not so much to equip young people with useful knowledge but to reimpose acceptance of bourgeois relations upon the unemployed. This is part of a process which can be observed in most institutions: the constantly repeated imposition of patterns of thinking and behaviour which individualize pupils to see themselves as individual citizens, consumers, employees and so on, categories which make it difficult for people to see themselves as part of a *class*.[7]

It is not surprising, then, that the most prevalent view about the state is that it is, indeed, above class. This opinion, which is associated with 'liberal democracy', was discussed in Chapter 4. It is held in this view that the state is neutral and therefore reasonable – merely reflecting back to us all the desires and values of 'society' as a whole. Popular will is expressed through the system of voting at elections, and so it is commonly believed that 'political democracy' provides the mechanisms by which rival interests and conflicts are reconciled.

Drawing upon the work of Marxist theorists, I have argued that the liberal-democratic model of the state is inadequate, and that we must recognize the fact that the state is increasingly identified with capital. The state is basically involved in sustaining the capitalist mode of production.

But how is the state to be conceptualized? I suggested that rather than thinking of 'the state in capitalist society', we should begin with 'the capitalist state approach'. I would want to argue that the Holloway-Picciotto thesis – that the state and its apparatuses, the law, the health service, education, etc., are a part of capitalist social relations – is basically correct. Education under capitalism is involved in the constant attempt to maintain its domination, state education serves the interest of capital by attempting to reproduce the technical and social relations of the capitalist mode of production, and the reproduction of the labour force.

The processes of reproduction and domination, however, are always uneven, complex, and contradictory. Let me give an example. It could be argued by many readers that the account in this book over-emphasizes the coercive elements, the shift towards the establishment of 'the strong state': the attempt to discipline the workers, to curb the rights of the trade unions, to provide strict regimes in Borstals for young offenders. Against this view, it could be said that I have neglected to describe the trend in the opposite direction: the attempts to *reduce* the power of the state. For example: the pruning of certain state institutions, the axing of some (minor) bureaucratic organizations, and the adoption, at certain times, of a so-called 'non-interventionist' policy. This tendency towards a reduction of state power shows itself in the field of education in a move towards (private) independent schooling, talk of local autonomy and 'parental choice'.

Though I would concede that there are both elements in the contradictions, I would maintain that the trend towards the strong state is the main one. There is, for example, a call for greater police powers, an extension of repressive law and stronger mechanisms of enforcement by senior police officers, who are increasingly intervening politically in civil rights issues. One of the implications of my view is that there is no point in the strategy of attempting to use the state against capital, because the state is increasingly becoming identified with capital. The growth of state activity represents a shift in the form of capitalist domination. There is now a crisis in the social relations of the domination of capital over labour, and so the state is attempting to restructure all its apparatuses, the law, health and social services – and the educational system. In other words, it is because of the crisis that the state is being forced to ensure a restructuring of educational provision.

In these chapters I have attempted to set some of the recent developments in education within the economic crisis of capitalism. It has been suggested that the trend towards the Right in British politics and the state is one response to the growing capitalist crisis. The forces and pressures that are being exerted on the political and economic levels are also being expressed in the field of education. In the chapters that follow it will be argued that the crisis is being utilized to create divisions within the working class – employed against unemployed, white against black, men against women – and that these divisions are expressed in education and need to be examined. It is difficult to struggle against some of these divisions, these discriminatory practices, such as racism and sexism, as they have become institutionalized. At the same time, social-democratic ideology tries to defuse the crisis by deploying 'neutral' categories such as consumers, citizens, customers, claimants, employees, and attempts to mobilize them. Let us now turn our attention to the problems of sexism and racism.

Chapter 7

Women and education

In this chapter my main concerns are to outline *the different perspectives* adopted by differing sections of the women's liberation movement; to introduce *the main debates* within the movement; and to examine *the socialization of girls* in schools, their ideological preparation for their roles in the economy. I will then place this discussion of *the sex divisions in education* within a larger context – that of *women's work*, paid and unpaid, within capitalism; and, finally, relate the problems of women's work to its cause: *the contradictions within capitalism itself*.

Introduction

Already by the 1870s some of the characteristics of contemporary education – such as the lack of child-care facilities and the division of the sexes (each specializing in different subjects) – were apparent. The 1870 Education Act had many important effects. Before it, many children were independent and proudly earning a living, according to Mayhew, at eight years of age, but after the passing of the Act, children did not have time to go out to work. I would suggest that the Education Act be seen as an intrusion, an attempt to control children's time by the state. This is an unusual view because much of the history of education is written from a middle-class point of view, and then generalized. There is a similar limitation in the traditional sociology of education which is dominated by a 'Durksonian' functionalism which decontextualizes and is ahistorical; it is a perspective that regards the status quo as natural, universal, necessary, unproblematic.

The ruling classes did not have an agreed view about the Education Act: there were different attitudes towards it which represented different interests. Most teachers saw themselves as a humanizing influence, and regarded schools as 'beacons of civilization' high above the squalid streets. Education did not merely impart information and knowledge, schools were civilizing agencies. With missionary zeal, the teachers instilled the values of cleanliness, self-respect, fear of God, love of country, obedience. It is interesting to note that in this period there were attempts to set up baby rooms and crèches, but that the authorities made them illegal. The ruling-class view was that mothers should be responsible for their children *at home*. The ideology of domesticity continues to pervade our society because it is not in the interests of capitalism to provide the facilities that could liberate women from domestic drudgery.

Boys and girls were taught separately and the education of girls was regarded as less important. After 1870, schools attendance officers were appointed, and though girls' absenteeism was much greater than the boys', it was the absenteeism of the boys that was regarded as serious. The content of girls' education (needlework and cookery), was preparation for a domestic role — a process which is still very widespread. The routeing of pupils on the basis of sex via typing of the curriculum will be discussed in a later section.

Masculinity and femininity, with their associated (stereotypical) characteristcs, are often seen as two distinct spheres. One feature of this ideology of the two spheres is the separation of work from home. At one time (craft) work and the family were closely related; they occupied the same space, but gradually a 'home' separate from the workplace became a sign of higher status. There is a close relationship between the ideological and the economic; for example, the ideology of domesticity is connected with marriage settlements. The latter often provided the necessary capital for the process of accumulation to begin. The development of commodity production meant that questions about linearity, inheritance, wealth became crucial issues.

Inspiration and drudgery

The importance of these concerns can be seen if one considers, for example, eighteenth- and nineteenth-century novels. It is possible to trace in them the beginnings of the ideology of domesticity and its development with the rise of the bourgeoisie. Some of the assumptions of this ideology are that women are intrinsically different from men. Women's main concern is the home; indeed, they have instincts and abilities which make them more fitted to be homemakers and child-rearers.

Through a careful reading of the novels of Jane Austen, Fanny Burney, the Brontës and Samuel Richardson, we can learn about how land became a commodity which the gentry monopolized. In principle one could buy land, but in practice entry was through *marriage* rather than purchase. In the novels of this period there are many references to marriage settlements, how sons inherited the estates, how the eldest son had the responsibility to provide for the widow, and so on. These elements show that romantic attachment was of less importance than economic relations. Material constraints acted on women and made them subordinate to their husbands. In economic terms, women stood to gain most through marriage — perhaps this accounts for the belief that women use sex to snare men. I mention the ideology of domesticity because it encapsulates all that the women's movement is against.

Capitalism and/or patriarchy

The contemporary women's liberation movement gathered force in the early 1960s; women became politicized and a radical critique developed. Many people became aware of the importance of consciousness and of what Fanon called 'the enemy outpost in one's head'. There was a call to uncover the 'hidden history of women'.[1] Women began to question the role of 'wife', 'mother', and rejected the passivity and dependence traditionally associated with those roles. Gradually, there was an increasing realization that those who did not 'go out to work', housewives, also worked; that pregnancy, breast-feeding, child-rearing was *work*. But this work is so often taken for granted that it is not seen, it is 'invisible'.

Research into these questions, the lives and preoccupations of women, is just beginning in and across many disciplines. Besides the political and economic studies, which compare capitalist societies with socialist ones, there are now an increasing number of historical and anthropological studies which compare contemporary capitalist societies with pre-capitalist ones.[2] Some historical research suggests that before capitalism, production was largely based in the home. With the development of large-scale commodity production and wage labour a separation occurred; the home and the factory became two distinct spheres. When capitalism required unskilled labour, men, women *and* children worked in the factories. Though some women have always worked (i.e. members of certain occupations or class segments) the convention was gradually established that females, generally, stayed at home. There were, of course, exceptions such as times of boom or war.

Historical studies vary so much in their interpretations that even a simple account such as the above is questioned. Radical feminists argue that capitalism did not make that much difference to women's oppression. Engels, however, argued that women's subordination did not exist before capitalism – and that capitalism caused it. It is not denied that there was a sexual division of labour before capitalism, the point is, capitalism took advantage of certain aspects of it. According to this view, the sexual division of labour is part of the social division of labour.

Little anthropological work has been done on the role and situation of women. Perhaps this is because there have been several problems to overcome. First, there is the problem of anthropologists seeing other societies through the rationality of their own culture. Second, most anthropologists in the past, being male, did not study the role of women; they interpreted other societies without examining their own presuppositions, their socialization, their taken-for-granted assumptions and interests. The work that has been done suggests that pre-capitalist societies were *not* all of the same type; some societies were matrilinear and others patrilinear.

Research crossing several subject areas has had a crucial part to play in the central debate within the women's movement. The question is: What is the relationship between capitalism and women's oppression? The theoretical analysis that is made of this issue is very important because different conceptions of political action will follow from it. There are two main approaches. One approach, or perspective, insists that women's oppression arises because of patriarchy, male supremacy. Writers who hold this position (such as Kate Millet, Shulamith Firestone, Christine Delphy) usually stress the point that patriarchy preceded capitalism, that it appears in all societies, and continues, even after the overthrow of private capital in the so-called 'socialist societies'.

The opposing approach argues that women's oppression is very closely related to capitalism – and so functional for it. Schematically, then, the main positions are these: 'radical feminists' believe that sex divisions are of more importance than class divisions. Marxist feminists believe either that class divisions are of more importance than sex divisions; or that sex and class divisions are interwoven together.[3] The women's movement is much more complex than this, but only these two broad factions will be considered here. That there can be no easy reconciliation between them is clear.

This can be seen in the case of the radical feminist Firestone, who believes that women's oppression derives from the sexual division of labour, their position as child-bearers within the family.[4] She wants to free women from their biology entirely by means of technology and therefore suggests the eradication of the family first through developing alternative lifestyles and eventually by reproducing people artificially, eliminating the female reproductive function. She is criticized by Marxist feminists who argue that she sees science and technology as autonomous, and ignores the nature and effects of capitalism. Socialist feminists argue that the sexual division is not the only one, that the oppression of women is not only a matter of biology but of class. They therefore want to link (despite the difficulties) the two concepts of 'sex' and 'class' together.[5]

Both these approaches analyse issues in very different ways; even the form in which problems are posed is dependent on the approach adopted. Consider, first, women's *unpaid* work, their labour in the home, domestic labour. Is this a form of organization, an expression of patriarchy, the domination of men over women, or is it a system by which capitalism reproduces the family and socializes its members? After all, the regeneration of the labour force is essential for capital.

But what about women's *paid* labour? Despite equal pay legislation differentials continue. There is still segregation between men's and women's jobs — the latter earning three-quarters of the men's wages. Again, one could argue that this is a product of sexism. Even in organizations such as trade unions, which are supposed to struggle on behalf of workers' interests, women workers are discriminated against by men. A Marxist approach to this question would tend to stress that such a labour force, weak and *divided*, is in the interests of capitalism. Women provide a reservoir of labour which can be sent back home (rather like 'guest-workers') when redundant to capitalist requirements. Such an analysis would be close to the position that contends that patriarchal relations and capitalist relations are not reducible to each other. (I will make some comments on this issue at the end of the chapter.) Patriarchy and capital are interlocked. The relationship of women and the state is mediated by men in the interests of capital. Its locus is the family.

The family and capitalism

Let us focus on the relationship between the family and capitalism. What is the relationship between the division of labour and the reproduction of the family?

The family household is based on kinship — but how functional is it for capitalism? I want to suggest that the division between men and women is formed in the family. There can be little doubt that capitalism seems to require a certain type of small, nuclear family — but what are its main features? The family/household system is one in which people share a wage. The family is used as the income/consumption unit. The cleaning, cooking, the servicing, all the (unpaid) work is done by the mother/wife in a privatized way. The small nuclear family is related to individualism. It is an institution into which women workers can dissolve when not needed in the factory. But more importantly, it is in such a family that labour power is produced for the capitalist – all that capitalism does it to ensure certain conditions. The family, then, is the institutional form for social reproduction, the reproduction of capitalism. The family is the place where personality structure is confirmed, training is provided; it is how the social formation is repaired day by day.[6] In all societies there is some provision for the aged and the ill, but under capitalism, there is also a necessity for the reproduction of the working class as a whole, for labour power.

Marxists point out that capitalist societies reproduce themselves through production relations, the division of labour, the social relations of production, and the sexual division of labour. After each cycle of production, the workers has only his/her labour power to sell again. The reproduction of labour power (of the future labour force) takes place in *the family*.

But radical feminists reject this view: they say that the family has nothing to do with capitalism, it is simply a form of patriarchy, domination by men. In their view, the oppression of women predates capitalism, but with the development of the capitalist mode of production the privatization of domestic labour has occurred. In the family, women are in relations of dependence to men.

And so, what should we do about the family? It is obviously within the family that socialization takes place. There is sexual conditioning into the roles of masculinity and femininity. It is such a privatized institution that it limits other forms of experiences. It imprisons people in a 'double-bind' and oppresses them. If this view is adopted, then it follows that the family should be subverted. But if we want to subvert it, what are the alternatives?

On the other hand, it is often said that though workers are alienated in the factory/market-place, the family 'compensates' for this, it provides a space for the development of individual uniqueness, for love, perhaps even the growth of an oppositional culture.[7] In this view, the family is often seen as a defensive institution against the intrusion of the state; this is why family life is often defended by the working class. The main problem is this: most of the working class do seem to support the family, but it is an institution based on the subordination of women. Should the family, then, be seen as an institution that should be subverted or should it be regarded as a base from which to attack capital? For the moment I will hold the question open until we have considered the following: Why does the state support the family (in the form of child benefits, old age benefits, etc.)? Why does the state increasingly intervene in the family and education? These are some of the issues we shall be analysing towards the end of this chapter.

But, first, let us examine the relationship between the family and education.

The socialization of girls in schools

What is the relationship between family and education, what Louis Althusser has called 'the family-education couple'? According to Althusser, the state has ideological state apparatuses (ISAs) and a repressive state apparatus that interlock. The ISAs include the educational system, the family, the media. Education, which has replaced the church as the dominant ISA, reproduces class relations and labour power, and the family prepares the worker for the factory every day. A weakness of the ISA thesis is that Althusser views the family in too homogeneous a way, without seeing its contradictory nature. Althusser can also be criticized for ignoring the feminist point of view.[8] But this is not unusual; Bowles and Gintis, though they too write of authority relationships, concern themselves with the inculcation of men but not of women. I will focus, therefore, particularly on sexual divisions in education.

Girls have higher educational attainments in the early years of schooling, but this initial advantage appears to wear off, and girls as a group leave school with fewer qualifications than boys and in a narrower range of subjects.[9] Why does this happen? One explanation is this: girls are socialized into familial and domestic roles and are denied certain forms of knowledge. Women's education provides an interesting case study in the sociology of knowledge, in that school knowledge, and by extension all knowledge, is divided into male and female knowledge. There is sex differentiation at the level of institutions and at the level of the curriculum. The education system divides pupils at an early age, and though the trend is towards mixed schooling, nearly a third of all schools are single-sex.

Using Bernstein's concepts of classification (the construction and maintenance of boundaries between different categories) and framing (the form and degree of control between teacher and taught), Madeleine MacDonald has written:[10]

> Given that a strong sexual division of labour exists within capitalism it is not surprising that the dominant gender code of schooling in Britain is that of strong classifications which reproduces the power relations of male-female hierarchy and strong framing where teachers play a large part in determining gender definition and control.

The existence of male-female hierarchy can be seen clearly at the level of the curriculum, most mixed schools providing different subjects for boys and girls. Certain types of knowledge are systematically offered or denied to pupils on the basis of sex. For example, fewer women have access to the scientific, technical mode of thought. (The other side of this phenomenon is the emphasis on fate and chance that plays such an important part in women's magazines.) The fact that boys are more likely to be offered the chance to study science subjects, and girls have more opportunity to study art and music, often produces restrictions at a later stage. In schools the arts/science dichotomy is thus a female/male distinction.[11]

Official government reports have consistently taken for granted that the interests of boys are related to their future occupational roles, whilst girls are concerned with their future roles as wives and mothers.[12]

If one studies the content of domestic science textbooks one finds the same assumptions: girls are taught that the home is a woman's primary responsibility. Women are defined as homemakers and mothers, thus girls are taught 'the duty and the privilege of serving one's family, subordination to the interests of husband and children, thrift and good management allied with tact and sympathy, good cooking and an attractive well-groomed appearance'.[13]

Thus the content and approach of textbooks enshrine sex as well as race and class stereotypes − but the school can hardly avoid the pervasive images of women that are current outside it. Even before girls come to school they have been bombarded with miniature domestic objects and toys socializing them for marriage, housework and child-rearing.[14] But it should be remembered that boys and girls do not only learn their roles through content but also through the form of the relationships they experience. The socialization of girls into subservient roles is apparent in books and films, in images and language, through ideology.[15]

The growth of higher education for women over the post-war boom has not broadened but has rather preserved the narrow range of women's employment. The most striking feature within higher and further education is that the choices of girls are severely restricted; they are consistently routed to more restrictive 'feminine' occupations. Whole areas of employment are predominantly female: nurses, typists, shop assistants, kitchen hands, hairdressers, telephone operators, clerks, cashiers, bartenders. In education, women form 67 per cent of the employed workforce.

But, of course, the majority of girls do not go on to higher or further education. Women emerge from the education system with qualifications at lower levels and in a more restricted range of subjects than boys. These factors ensure women's eventual over-representation in the part-time and unskilled sectors of the labour market. The superior prestige of abstract and pure knowledge both mirrors and legitimates the dominance of intellectual over manual labour.

To sum up this section: women reproduce children physically *and* ideologically mainly within the context of the family. Women as mothers are socializers of their children. But *most teachers are women* and are also the chief agents of early school socialization. The school continues the ideological function of socialization into work identity for men, and work/family, identity for women. Women are ideologically prepared for service roles within the family, and the subordinate roles they occupy in social production. In education sexual divisions are perpetuated and reproduced.[16] I described some of the practices through which discrimination is continued and the notion transmitted that women are not just different but subordinate. The ruling ideology is thus reproduced in a material way. I am arguing that schools are not really vehicles for social mobility, but a means of reproducing the structure of class and patriarchal relationships. The social democratic ideology of 'equality of opportunity' masks the real processes that are taking place in the educational system. In reality, the educational system performs the functions of socialization, differentiation, distribution and stratification. The household work performed by women in the family is essential for the maintenance of the labour force engaged in production. Schools, by recreating the division of labour, ensure the reproduction of the relations of production. The educational system thus meshes with capital to ensure the maintenance of women's oppression. In the next section I will analyse two aspects of that oppression that mutually reinforce each other: social labour in the office/factory and privatized, domestic labour in the home.

The position of women in capitalist society

This section is an analysis, grounded in a study of Marxist economics, of the material basis of women's oppression under capitalism.

The oppression of women under capitalism lies in their dual role. Women as domestic workers perform work in the home which is necessary for capital. This work is outside social production. At the same time, women occupy an inferior position in social production. These two aspects of women's oppression mutually reinforce each other.[17] This has not always been the case. Only under capitalism do women perform two types of labour, social labour in the factory and privatized labour in the home. In pre-capitalist collective societies, before the existence of private property and class society, household tasks were an integral part of social production. Engels argues that the sexual division of labour within the family did not assign an inferior role to women.[18] He writes that it was the factory system and the development of commodity production that brought about the separation of privatized work in the home from social production in the factory. It is because women are forced to perform both domestic work *and* wage labour that their position in social production remains unequal. Let me clarify this.

The sole aim of capitalism is the accumulation of capital. The worker sells to the capitalist her capacity to labour. In the capitalist mode of production labour power, not labour, is the commodity that the capitalist buys. If the worker sold herself she would be a slave, but she sells labour power, which belongs for a certain period of time to the capitalist. This commodity, labour power, is the only commodity that has the property of creating more value than it possesses itself. The separation of labour power from the labourer is inherent in the process of capitalist production. At the end of the working day the worker must leave the production process in order to replenish what previously the capitalist employer had consumed – the labour power – so that this commodity can be sold again the following day. The replenishment of the capacity to labour takes place through *the individual consumption of the worker*.

Now, two sorts of consumption take place in capitalist society: there is *productive consumption* of labour power that takes place within social production, and there is *individual consumption* of the worker in replenishing labour power, which requires labour time, outside social production. Individual consumption, in short, is to replenish the worker's labour power. The sustenance of the worker requires labour and toil; there is shopping and cooking, washing and ironing, cleaning and repairing to be done; there is child-care and countless other tasks to be performed. It falls upon the working class, and women in particular, to carry out this labour for itself.

There is a controversial issue here: is domestic work productive or unproductive? It will be remembered that productive labour is labour exchanged with capital and engaged in the production of surplus value. Unproductive labour is paid not by capital but out of revenue. Domestic work is concrete labour which lies outside the capitalist production process and therefore cannot produce surplus value.[19] It follows that domestic work, since it involves neither an exchange with capital nor revenue, is therefore neither productive nor unproductive labour. Domestic work, whilst a necessary condition to the reproduction of capital, nevertheless remains outside of social production as privatized toil in the home. Since no surplus value can be produced by domestic work, capital has no interest in its socialization (i.e. in making it social).

This debate, which may seem abstract and somewhat academic, was important for several reasons: it focused attention on women's work in the family and was a feminist challenge to Marxism. The domestic labour debate stressed the fact that women were exploited by capital; it left untouched, however, the question of sexual subordination.

Women and the reserve army of labour

I have argued that the perpetuation of domestic work performed gratis for capital means not only that women are domestic toilers but also that they exist for capital as a cheap, unorganized source of labour. Let me now, briefly, outline some of the characteristics of women's paid employment, and the theories used to understand them. The first characteristic feature to note is that there is job segregation: women predominate in the clothing, footware, food, drink and textile industries, in banking and insurance, in the *service* occupations. There is ghettoization into certain occupations.

Second, while the number of full-time women workers has fallen, the number of part-timers has increased. Part-time work is womens work. It is not shown in official statistics; moreover, as there is no clear definition of 'part-time', the number of hours worked varies tremendously. Many women are forced to do part-time work at home (for example, Asian women in the clothing industry). Many women have to work not just for 'pin-money' but often to maintain the household. Women occupy a contradictory position as part-time workers in that they are easier to make redundant and yet, at the same time, are more productive and cheaper to employ for the capitalist. By increasing part-time opportunities for women, employers are avoiding some of the economic consequences of the law. Moreover, the growth of part-time jobs is actually a barrier to the realization of equal pay for women. It is hard to compare the similarity of part-time jobs because there are so few men in part-time employment.

Three theories are commonly used in the discussion of women's paid labour. The traditional viewpoint, often held by international organizations and expressed in government reports, is called 'women's two-roles theory'. It is largely concerned with the notion of married women working and with the implications of this for relationships within the family. Many studies were based on this theory.[20] Taking the concept of sex-role for granted, the theory emphasizes the tension between the two roles, housewife and worker, it stresses the role-conflict that the working wife may experience. The taken-for-granted assumptions of this theory are such that some questions are just not asked: which jobs are filled by men and which jobs are filled by women? Why are there such great differences between men's and women's jobs? In other words, there is no structural analysis of the ways the capitalist labour process structures the organization of work and the demand for labour. There is no analysis of the conditions which give rise to the sexual division of labour.

Second, there is the 'dual labour market' theory which states that there are two sectors, the primary sector and the smaller, secondary sector, the employers of which have different strategies to cope with workers. Primary sector jobs have high earnings, a high degree of security, good opportunities for promotion, while secondary jobs have relatively low earnings, little job security, negligible opportunities for promotion. Primary employees are more likely to be mobile within hierarchically organized career structures, while secondary employees tend to move between occupations, in and out of unskilled and semi-skilled jobs. In this approach it is argued that there are certain attributes which make a particular group likely to be a source of secondary workers, and that women possess them. Women have a relatively low inclination to acquire valuable training and experience, are easily dispensable, do not rate economic rewards highly and so forth. This theory is inadequate because the 'attributes' which women are said to possess are based on stereotypes; indeed, the form of explanation is tautological. Moreover, there is no analysis of women's role in the family and of the labour process.

Third, there is the orthodox Marxist theory which I have already outlined in the discussion on the labour process. In short, it argues that capitalism subordinates the labour process to its control as there is a move from manufacture to large-scale industry, from absolute to relative surplus value.[21]

Gradually, the work rhythm and work content of living labour are subordinated to the mechanical needs of machinery itself. Machines are capital's main weapon for subordinating labour to capital. Machines not only increase the production of relative surplus-value; they also create a 'reserve army of labour'. Women enter the labour force as low-paid workers both to do jobs which have been deskilled by mechanization, and also to work in labour-intensive sectors. They can be drawn into or thrown out of employment according to the needs of capital accumulation. At the present time more and more women are being thrown back into the home, but why is this? To answer this question it may be useful at this point to provide a recapitulation of the reasons for the economic crisis.

As capital accumulation develops, increases in the productivity of labour are expressed by a rise in the organic composition of capital. That is to say, more capital is invested as constant capital, on machinery and raw materials, than is paid out as wages for productive workers. Now, profits arise out of the exploitation of workers alone but the rate of profit is measured over the total capital invested and not just that invested in labour power. So that, as productivity increases, there are relatively fewer workers exploited by a given amount of capital and there is a larger cost of machinery, etc., over which to measure the rate of profit. This means that there is a tendency for the rate of profit to fall. Here we have the main contradiction of capitalism: the expansion of capital is based on increases in productivity, but it is just these increases in productivity which tend to bring about a fall in the rate of profit.

The capitalist crisis is both the expression of the contradiction of capitalism of the fall in the rate of profit, *and* of the way that capitalism attempts to resolve these contradictions internally. One of the most important ways in which capital attempts to resolve the crisis is by the increase in the reserve army of labour (the unemployed) which puts capital in a stronger position to restore profitability by attempting to drive down wages below the value of labour power.

As the capitalist crisis gains momentum, women are being greatly affected. Most of the 'cuts' are taking place in the unproductive state sector, in health and education, which is largely staffed by women.[22] More and more women are being thrown back into the home, to the privatized, unpaid drudgery of domestic work. It is not surprising to see that capital is trying to make staying at home the respectable norm, it is a part of its ideological offensive. Unemployment and inflation have made it imperative to convince women that their place is in the home. And so the care of old people by their female kin is increasing; women are being encouraged to look after physically and mentally handicapped people at home. All this justifies women's lack of participation in productive work. As more and more responsibility is being placed on women in the home, one wonders whether the discussions about 'self-help' in the media are entirely a coincidence?

Sexual division and class exploitation

I shall now make some brief remarks on the problematic relationship between sexual division and class exploitation. I do this because it is one of the most important unresolved issues within the women's movement. Many people feel that as Marxism always stresses class the women's question has been marginalized. It is said that Marxism has no vocabulary with which to talk about sexual division; it does not deal with sexual politics.

Some recent work, influenced by radical feminism, emphasizes this and suggests that men gain material advantages from the oppression of women. Christine Delphy in *The Main Enemy* focuses on women's labour within marriage, and states that some are not given a wage for their domestic work, but only their 'keep'.[23] If one strips away the notions of love and romance, one sees that women are like slaves provided for by a master. What sustains this situation is the marriage contract. The author asserts that in contemporary society there are two modes of production, an industrial and a patriarchal one. These modes are distinct and autonomous, and in terms of the patriarchal/domestic mode of production women constitute a distinct *class*, united by their common oppression by men. She concludes that women should mobilize autonomously to overthrow patriarchy and the society in which it is embedded.

In an analysis which has some similarities with Delphy's, Heidi Hartmann has suggested that both capitalism and Marxism are sex-blind.[24] For capitalists, as long as surplus value is extracted, it does not matter very much whether it is men or women that are exploited. For Marxists, the concept of the reserve army of labour, for example, is a useful term, but it does not explain why it is women rather than men that are most affected in a recession. She argues that there is a marriage between the interests of capital and the interests of men; that is to say, capitalism makes use of sex antagonisms, though it is not their cause.

Though sympathetic to the above argument, I have a few reservations about some of the groups within the women's movement. I believe that *one* of the tendencies within radical feminism developed at a time of economic boom, from the faction of educated petit-bourgeois women who were denied equality in education and job opportunities with men. The bourgeois character of some radical feminist groups is partly a result of its middle-class following. As they see men as the perpetuators of female oppression, and champion the interest of the female sex rather than the working class, their strategy is to fight for 'equal rights' — but they do so within the framework of capitalism.[25] They feel things should be 'fairer', in other words, they want reforms within the present economic system rather than revolutionary change. Radical feminists have an anti-male approach and wish to organize themselves autonomously and separately from any other oppressed group. I believe that this separation leads to fragmentation and has a demobilizing effect.

Radical feminists correctly stress the importance of language personality and sexuality as elements in women's oppression. But their analyses often lack a historical dynamic because these concepts are not related to the capitalist mode of production.

Let me now summarize this chapter. I began by showing that the sexist characteristic of contemporary education was built into the whole design of 'mass' education. The content of girls' education was, as it still is today, preparation to be a wife and mother, cook and housekeeper. This 'ideology of domesticity', reflected in the literature of the period, is connected with the development of commodity production. I asked the question: are women oppressed by patriarchy or by capitalism? The main positions, radical feminism and socialist feminism, were distinguished, and there was a consideration of women's unpaid and paid labour from these contrasting points of view.

I then focused on the family, the various functions it performs, and the relationship between the family and education. It was suggested that girls are systematically denied certain types of knowledge and socialized into passive, subservient roles. Then followed an analysis of two aspects of women's oppression that mutually reinforce each other: social labour in the office/factory and privatized domestic labour in the home. This is the dual role for which girls are ideologically prepared by the schools. Domestic labour was explained by individual consumption – the need to replenish the workers' labour power. Whilst it is a necessary condition for the reproduction of capital, domestic work produces no surplus value.

After an outline of some of the characteristics of women's paid employment there was a discussion of how capitalism subordinates the labour process to its control, how mechanization not only increases the production of surplus value but also creates a 'reserve army of labour'. The main thrust of the argument was that the schooling of girls, its links with the structures of women's oppression, can only be fully understood by a recognition of the contradictions within capitalism itself.

In this chapter I have tried to show that the oppression of women is rooted in capitalist relations of production, that women's inequality is perpetuated by capital partly through the education system which performs the functions of socialization, differentiation, distribution, and stratification. It is in schools that girls are ideologically prepared for service roles within the family and the subordinate roles they occupy in social production. Schools are not vehicles for large-scale mobility, but a means of reproducing the structure of class relationships. Schools recreate the division of labour *in complex and contradictory ways*, and thus ensure the reproduction of the relations of production. The educational system thus meshes with capital to ensure the maintenance of women's oppression.

When girls become women, capital places a double burden on them as wage workers and child-rearers. They perform the essential tasks of child-bearing and child-rearing gratis. Moreover, women are a source of cheap labour, called upon to work in the factory or sent back into the home according to capital's needs. This is how capital benefits from the oppression of women.

But that is not all the story. There are undoubtedly real material conflicts between men and women. As Mary McIntosh has put it:[26]

> Capitalist society is one in which men as men dominate women; yet it is not this but class domination that is fundamental to the society. It is a society in which the dominant class is composed mainly of men; yet it is not as men but as capitalists that they are dominant.

Capital has built its own divisions on to already existing sexual divisions, a patriarchal division of labour has been 'taken over' and adapted by the structures of capital.

It has to be conceded that orthodox Marxism has dealt inadequately with women's subordination. In the past there has been a tendency in political economy to focus only on abstract economic categories, on 'capital-logic'. Many feminists have felt that the political parties do not deal sufficiently with personal oppression. For many women, the personal is the political and they want to stress the richness of people's lived experience and the necessity of new forms of organization.[27] Marxist theory has paid insufficient attention, until recently, to the issue of patriarchy, and the ways in which sexual divisions and intra-class divisions interrelate. The implication of the feminist challenge is that Marxism will have to be further developed, transformed.

Chapter 8

Race, imperialism and education

Introduction

This chapter begins by placing the use of immigrant labour in the context of the needs of capital. And as the majority of foreign workers in advanced European countries are drawn from nations systematically underdeveloped by imperialism, there is then an exploration of the relationship between capitalism and imperialism. Imperialism oppresses immigrant labour in many ways, including discrimination.

The second section makes a link between the economic and ideological levels of racism. It shows how biology is being used ideologically to legitimize racist attitudes and practices at a time of capitalist crisis. The third section is a consideration of the forms of discrimination within education. There is a discussion of the features of the 'assimilationist' model, which was applied to the first generation of immigrants, and the shift to the current 'multi-cultural' model. It is argued that as the latter model operates without an economic and political analysis of what racism is, its strategies are inadequate.

Immigrant labour and imperialism

What are the key features of the present race situation? A race situation implies an economic and political conflict. Second, there is a restriction of social mobility for the oppressed race. Third, dominant social structures are supported by ideologies and the status quo is justified by deterministic legitimations.[1] As the terms racialism and racism are now often used interchangeably, let me make my own usage clear: racialism refers to feelings of prejudice and its justification, racism is the systematic practice of discrimination by the institutions of the state. To understand racialism and racism fully we need to

93

look at the relationship between immigrant labour and imperialism.

Britain, immediately after the Second World War, went through a period of extremely rapid economic growth. Like most other Western European countries, Britain was faced with *a chronic shortage of labour*. But it was in a position to turn to an alternative source of labour: its colonies and ex-colonies in Asia, Africa and the West Indies. These underdeveloped regions had a large labour force, but no capital with which to make the labour productive. It was to these vast and cheap resources of labour that Britain turned in the 1950s. The following points should be remembered: as the first major capitalist power to dominate the world, British imperialism has a lengthy history of utilizing immigrant labour. Second, it suited Britain to import the workers it needed, as it was the quickest way of getting the cheapest labour at minimum cost. The shortage of workers, *at that time*, made immigrants economically acceptable.

During this post-war expansion white workers were moving into more skilled jobs and out of manufacturing into the service sector. There were certain jobs the white workers steered away from. And so, in the 1950s, immigrant labour was brought in to do the very worst jobs. The immigrants came to the major urban areas and filled jobs which white workers did not want, jobs which meant low earnings, working in unpleasant conditions and unsocial hours.[2]

By 'working unsocial hours' I am referring to shift work. With increasing mechanization in the 1950s and 1960s there was a rise in shift working to enable machinery to be worked intensively. The concentration of black workers in shift working is very high particularly in food manufacture (bakeries), the clothing, hotel and catering industries, brick and metal manufacture (foundries), car/vehicle manufacture, the National Health Service, and public transport.

British capitalism takes advantage of immigrants in order to help maintain the rate of profit: first, by the provision of supplying labour to do the worst jobs at low wages under poor conditions; second, by permitting shift working. Immigrant labour, then, is a special kind of labour brought to Britain to be exploited in a specific way.[3] Capitalism has not arbitrarily developed a low-paid sector, shift work, etc.; these are necessary features of capitalism. But what is the relationship between capitalism and imperialism? And are racism and imperialism inseparable?

It may be useful at this point to indicate how capitalism has grown into a world system of colonial oppression, and how in its economic essence imperialism *is* monopoly capitalism. Lenin's pamphlet *Imperialism, The Highest Stage of Capitalism* is one of the most significant and insightful writings of this century.[4] Though written in 1916, it is amazingly contemporary — and therefore relevant.

Lenin believed that it was impossible to understand modern war and politics without understanding the question of imperialism. His argument is this: there has been an enormous growth of industry and the concentration of production in ever-larger enterprises. The concentration of production has resulted in a rise of monopolies. They come to an agreement on the conditions of sale; they divide the markets among themselves; they fix the quantity of goods to be produced. They fix the prices – and then divide the profits.

The banks have also combined into powerful cartels. The original function of banks was to serve middlemen in the making of payments, but they now influence capitalists by facilitating or hindering credit. According to Lenin, banks greatly intensify and accelerate the process of concentration of capital and the formation of monopolies. Banks have developed into the monopolists of finance capital, and these syndicates inevitably penetrate into every sphere of public life. Industrial capitalists have become completely dependent on the banks. There is, then, a coalescence of bank and industrial capital as the banker is transformed, to an ever-increasing degree, into an industrial capitalist. Thus the twentieth century marks the turning point from free competition to monopoly, from the domination of capital in general to the domination of *finance* capital.

Typical of the old capitalism, when free competition was the rule, was *the export of goods*; typical of the new capitalism, when monopolies rule, is *the export of capital*. Lenin writes:[5]

> surplus capital will be utilized not for the purpose of raising the standard of living of the masses in a given country, for this would mean a decline in profits for the capitalists, but for the purpose of increasing profits by exporting capital abroad to the backward countries. In these backward countries profits are usually high, for capital is scarce, the price of land is relatively low, wages are low, raw materials are cheap.

In these international transactions the creditor always secures some advantage, an extra benefit, and he is more firmly attached to the debtor than the seller to the buyer. As the export of capital increases, finance capital begins the division of the world. This is the highest stage of capitalism. Imperialism is the epoch of monopolies and finance capital; in its economic essence imperialism *is* monopoly capitalism.

There is a desperate struggle for colonies, the final partition of the world. Many countries, even though they are officially independent, become enmeshed in the net of financial and diplomatic dependence. Capitalism grows into a world system of colonial oppression.

Let me now make the link between imperialism and immigrant labour. Lenin stated that the development of capitalism into imperialism is a necessary and inevitable development of the essential tendencies of capitalist production. The world is divided up into colonies, 'spheres of influence', by the advanced countries for whom the export of capital has become more important than the export of commodities. Imperialism created the conditions where workers are faced with the choice of staying in the 'periphery' and barely subsisting or else migrating to the metropolitan centres in search of work.

By the terms 'periphery' and 'metropolitan' I am referring to the advanced capitalist nations (the metropolises) that exploit the less advanced countries.[6] The increasing wealth of the metropolis has its necessary counterpart in the decreasing wealth of the periphery: When the capitalists in the imperialist nations need to expand their labour force they must do this without undermining profitability, and they therefore turn to the international reserve army for cheap labour to perform the worst jobs. The overwhelming majority of foreign workers in advanced European countries are drawn from nations systematically underdeveloped by imperialism. International migration is vital to imperialism; capitalism needs this reserve army of labour not only to allow uninterrupted accumulation, but also to control the level of wages.

All capitalists benefit from the exploitation of immigrant labour in Britain, just as all capitalists in South Africa benefit from apartheid. Black people in this country form a special and oppressed section within the British working class; black people are a sub-proletariat, a new dark-skinned underclass beneath the white social order. Black and immigrant workers suffer specific racial oppression over and above the normal oppression and exploitation experienced by all workers. Race and racial discrimination are inherent in British capitalism. Racism serves the needs of capitalist profitability.[7] Racism and imperialism are inseparable.

Capitalist accumulation and racist ideology

In the last few years capitalism has faced its worst economic crisis since the Second World War. One of the effects of this crisis is the great increase in unemployment – particularly amongst black youth. At the same time, it can be noticed that in the media there is an increasing emphasis on the defence of one's territory against 'outsiders', and attention has been focused on aggressive behaviour by white groups against 'the foreigners'. This section attempts to show the links between these phenomena, how a biological ideology accompanies and relates to a particular *economic* situation.

I begin by recapitulating the capitalist accumulation process, the imperative to increase surplus value which leads to the continual introduction of new technology. I do this because this process leads to an increase in the reserve army of labour, which is not required in a time of crisis. It will be then argued that certain aspects of ethology and sociobiology are being popularized to legitimize racism.

Capitalist production has as its aim and driving force the production of the greatest amount of surplus value. (Surplus value, you may remember, is the difference between the exchange value of labour power and its productive capacity.) Capital, in its necessity to increase the wealth it produces, has two main methods: absolute surplus value and relative surplus value. Absolute surplus value is an increase in the rate of surplus value by lengthening or intensifying the working day. But capital soon comes up against the fact that the normal working day has its physical and moral limits.

After the working day has been lengthened to these limits there is only one way capital can increase surplus value. This is through an emphasis on relative surplus value, through a decrease in the portion of a given working day devoted to necessary labour. (Necessary labour is that part of the working day in which the worker produces the equivalent of his own means of subsistence.) In other words, there is a transition from the production of absolute surplus value (extension of the working day) to that of relative surplus value, which is shortening the part of the working day necessary to produce the wages of the workers. To put this in another way, there is a decrease in the necessary part of the working day by an increase in the social productivity of labour.

Though capital attempts to reduce the necessary labour time to a minimum by increasing the productivity of labour, there are also physical and moral limits to the increase in the intensity of labour. The main method open for advanced capitalist countries to increase surplus value is to increase productivity through the introduction of new machinery.[8] There is a compulsion to increase the productivity of labour and to reduce the cost of production by the utilization of new technology.

In Marx's words, capital increases the scale of production through the replacing of living labour (variable capital) by objectified, dead labour in the form of machinery (constant capital). The capitalist who introduces the new machinery undercuts others, and makes an extra profit. The increase in the investment in machinery, in turn, increases the productivity of labour. There is fierce competition and a cheapening of commodities. The imperative to increase surplus value leads to an incessant revolutionizing of technology. The constantly increasing quantity of the means of production, with the decrease in the labour power required leads to the formation of what

Marx called the industrial reserve army, the unemployed. The process described above is what Marx called the absolute general law of capitalist accumulation.

It is through the continual introduction of new technology, then, that capital produces a reserve army of labour. Now, the size of the reserve army, the unemployed, is relative to the rate of capital accumulation. More accumulation means an increase in the proletariat. In a time of economic crisis, however, the reserve army is not required, unemployment increases, *blacks and women are sent 'home'. For both these groups there are accompanying ideologies.*[9]

We are now witnessing campaigns asserting the value of 'family life'; women are being told of the importance of staying at home in order to provide a secure, loving environment for their young children. The writings of John Bowlby are being given increasing coverage in the media.[10] It seems to me that this is an ideological aspect of current state policies towards the family. State policies are based on certain assumptions about the nature of 'normal' family relationships which impose on women the responsibility of caring for children and elderly relatives.[11] In this way social policies implicitly legitimize the role of women as unpaid domestic workers.

Black people are also being sent 'home' from the workplace. The attendant ideology of this tendency is racism. I want to argue that the new style of 'scientific racism' that is emerging is based on a reductionist biology and utilizes ethology and sociobiology. But, first, what is 'scientific racism'? By 'scientific racism' is meant any claim of the natural superiority of one identifiable human population, group or race over another. In recent years there have been attempts to use the concepts and techniques of science in support of theories that claim that some particular groups are innately inferior to others in terms of 'intelligence' or 'culture'. It is this ideological use of science that is called 'scientific racism'.[12]

The popularization of ethology

There are many forms of biologism, but for the purpose of exposition and analysis I will discuss here only ethology and sociobiology. Ethologists like Niko Tinbergen and Konrad Lorenz study the patterns of behaviour of animals in their natural environment. Ethology emphasizes the careful observation of as many species as possible, and there is a tendency to interpret behaviour as the result of evolution moulded by natural selection.

The views of ethologists have been popularized by writers such as Robert Ardrey and Desmond Morris.[13] In his book *The Naked Ape*,

Morris asserts that human conduct is most fruitfully interpreted, predicted and controlled in the light of studies of other primates. He often uses analogies between baboons and human beings and assumes that there is a significant parallel between the two categories. Robert Ardrey, in the book *Territorial Imperative*, makes claims for the innate aggressiveness of human beings and their urge to possess territory. The usual strategy of these writers is to give a description of a group of animals, and then a description of a human characteristic in much the same terms. Alternatively, we are told about a problem in grasping human behaviour genetically, and then a non-human species is indicated by means of which an explanation might be possible.[14]

Ethologists attempt to show that the existence of innate instincts is genetic in origin, that significant biological drives determine human behaviour. Lorenz, for example, roots all behaviour in the drives of feeding, reproduction, defence and flight. The areas of 'instinctual' behaviour that are most commonly focused upon are aggression and the guarding of territory; we are told that human behaviour exhibits 'aggression' or 'territoriality' and that the root cause of aggression is competition for resources. Territoriality establishes monopoly rights over resources within a portion of usable space. Another way of regulating competition is through hierarchy; this, it is said, creates an order of precedence in access to, and distribution of, resources. The rationalization of these views — *the defence of one's own territory, the justification of aggressive behaviour on behalf of one's own group against outsiders* — has gained sophistication in recent years through the contribution of sociobiology.

The contribution of sociobiology

Sociobiologists, like Edward Wilson and Richard Dawkins, argue that selfishness characterizes evolution.[15] All human behaviour is genetically based and is ultimately selfish. We are temporary, disposable, gene machines; our genes make brief use of us, then cast us aside:[16]

> A gene which makes its successive bodies behave altruistically towards just any Tom, Dick or Harry will not be a successful gene. But now consider a gene which makes its bodies behave altruistically towards only close relatives, say by sharing food with a brother, or saving him from danger. Since there is a good chance that an identical copy of the very same gene is sitting in the body of the relative saved, there is a good chance that the gene for kin-altruism is saving itself . . . This is why mothers protect and feed their children, often at crippling cost to themselves. Genes manipulate

mothers to benefit replicas of those same genes in children.

Survival, then, is selfish. The genes may dictate that the body learn from its environment, but the logic of survival remains: the aim and rationale of all behaviour is always the onward transmission of genes. The body is a 'gene machine', a throwaway survival machine for our selfish and immortal genes:[17]

> A selfish gene is the opposite of an altruistic gene, and an altruistic gene is defined as one which has the effect of increasing the chances of survival of a rival gene, at the expense of its own. By definition an altruistic gene propagates fewer copies of itself than its selfish rival. Therefore, automatically, the genes whose effects we see manifested in living bodies are selfish genes.

Let me summarize the version of human nature presented by ethology and sociobiology: human behaviour is naturally selfish and territorial; this naturalness is rooted in our genetic make-up. We would not have survived until now were it not for our having these characteristics. The drive is for survival. A culture is a system of learned responses, limited and shaped by genetic requirements; naturally and instinctively a group will seek to defend its own culture. The more closely related individuals are, the more likely one is to act altruistically on the others' behalf. For example, an animal sacrificing its life for members of its own family is actually improving the chances that genes like its own will survive. Thus it is argued that the greater the internal bond within a group the greater the external aggression. In short, altruism is directed primarily towards one's closest relatives — and against the outgroup. Hostility to outsiders is, therefore, endemic and natural. And, because certain features are genetic, however much the environment is altered, the genetic characteristics are immovable and permanent. This is the type of explanation given to justify territorial defence behaviour and aggression, and which is expressed in racialism.

Sociobiologists stress the continuity between the natural and the social; Dawkins, for example, juxtaposes the social kingdom with the animal kingdom. But facts and conclusions about animal behaviour cannot necessarily be generalized and applied to human behaviour. Moreover, altruism and selfishness are value-laden terms. And so the questions I want to ask are these: Can we argue by analogy in this way? Second, if genes are selfish, how can we explain unselfish behaviour? Could conditions be set up socially for the survival of altruism? It seems to me that though sociobiologists state that they are dealing only with facts, their work is based on a deterministic view of human nature, which is presented to us as a description. Their views are being used to justify theories of racial oppression, male superiority, and class domination.

Some right-wing organizations, like the National Front, actually propagate the view that the nation is a family: the national family is the organic whole within which the individual contributes to its survival. It is argued by supporters of the National Front that man (sic) and society are the creation of 'man's' biological nature; the behaviour and social organization are determined to a crucial extent by genetic inheritance. They insist that genetic inheritance determines inequality, not social environment. As for Western 'man's' abstract, 'intellectual' notions of equality and the oneness of the species (notions which threaten his survival), these are in direct conflict with the promptings of 'his' inherited instinct.[18]

Biologism as an ideology

Problems of the social order are often displaced by a biological 'rationale'. It is well-known that biologism was a legitimator of the social order in the nineteenth century. Both the class structure at home and imperialist expansion abroad were justified under the name of Social Darwinism. In the present period of social crisis, biologism is being used once again.

As a theoretical model, biologism is a form of that reductionism which is the dominant paradigm of contemporary science. For biologism, all the richness of human experience and the varying historical forms of human relationships merely represent the product of underlying biological structures. In a word, the human condition is reduced to mere biology. The work of both ethologists and sociobiologists has been used to popularize the view that intellectual, cultural and moral qualities are genetically transmitted, and that certain groups can be graded as inferior. Legitimation for conserving the social order is provided by the dominance hierarchy ('pecking order') studies in ethology. It is then implied that stratification is not associated with specific societies and culture but reflects a genetically laid-down necessity. Male dominance and female passivity, male aggression and female domesticity are understood to have a biological basis. But, as Steven and Hilary Rose have pointed out, research which may provide an elegant account of certain aspects of animal behaviour is displaced into a total account of the whole human condition: 'Scarcely surprisingly, if humans are interpreted as ill-suppressed bundles of aggressive instincts, the formulation for social policy relates to control rather than liberation.'[19] In biologism, economic and sociological accounts of social structure thus become diminished to the working out of the evolutionary imperative. In these accounts biology is invoked to explain away sociology.

Biologism has become a vehicle for an anti-Marxist ideology which stresses not only aggressive instincts but also economic competitiveness. The ideas of Adam Smith with their stress on self-help, self-interest are being revived and given a so-called biological validity. It is said that we are always seeking to better ourselves at the expense of our peers; that we have a powerful drive to fight in order to survive and so the concept of 'enemy' is deeply imprinted in our genes. I have already mentioned Robert Ardrey's work, which has been used to show that instincts are the products of evolution from our earliest human beginnings. The competitive instinct is an example of an instinct which has a direct influence upon class stratification, separating the 'bright', the 'talented', the 'leaders' from the rest. Social classes are thus seen as genetic groupings. It is an easy slide to the fascist position of the National Front who assert that 'the basic instinct common to all species is to identify only with one's like group, to in-breed and to shun out-breeding. In human society this instinct is racial.'[20]

In the above section I have attempted to interconnect base and superstructure, the economic and ideological 'levels', 'to hold the two ends of the chain together'. I outlined the general law of capital accumulation and stated that in a time of economic crisis the reserve army of labour increases and is not required. The living standards of the working class are attacked and large sections of it, beginning with women and blacks, are thrown out of the labour process. I argued that for both these groups there are attendant ideologies. For women, the ideology of domesticity, 'family life', the care of the young, the old, is enforced by state policies.

To contain the blacks there is the ideology of 'racism'. Capitalism's struggle for survival has made it necessary and possible to recruit biologism as the generator of ideologies which are firmly locked into the processes of social control. I have argued that biologism, particularly ethology and sociobiology, provide ideological support for the legitimation and justification of certain policies associated with the deepening economic crisis of capitalism. Racism is a structural category which legitimates the existing order and, at the same time, creates divisions within the working class: Such an ideology is clearly perceived when articulated by right-wing organizations, but when these ideological beliefs become gradually institutionalized by the state and expressed in state policies, they tend to become accepted as the 'norm', a part of lived 'common sense'. But 'common sense', as Gramsci reminded us, is the practical ideology of the ruling classes — those classes which have learned to represent their ideas as 'the only rational, universally valid ones'.

Discrimination in education

My main argument is that imperialism oppresses immigrant labour and that this oppression takes many forms. Besides biologism which is one form of oppression, racism is expressed through formal legal mechanisms and the maintenance of discrimination.[21] There is an overwhelming mood of anger amongst black people about this discrimination. They have grievances about education, employment, the law, the police, prisons, immigration procedures, and the lack of black political representation. In this section I want to focus on racism within schools and the inadequacies of the current 'multicultural education' model.

The assimilationist model

During the 1960s 'multiracial education' was understood in terms of blacks themselves being the 'problem'. Much concern was expressed about their *numbers*, the concentration of immigrant pupils in particular schools and areas. The concentration of black people, the development of foreign enclaves within British culture and society, was seen as a threat. It was suggested by the government that once a school or class became more than one third immigrant 'serious strains' arose. This was the justification for the adoption of policies of dispersal.

Dispersal policies, which were carried out by bussing or changing catchment areas (zoning), discriminated against black pupils and institutionalized racism. Black children were bussed irrespective of whether they had special educational needs or not. No consideration was given to the fact that bussing militated against the involvement of children in their own communities and the formation of neighbourhood friendships. Though bussing is not so widely practised as it was in the 1960s and early 1970s, the concern with concentration, the 'ideology of numbers' is still widely prevalent.[22]

Besides the number and concentration of black immigrants, attention was also focused on their language 'problem'. The organization of language teaching augmented racist and discriminatory practices. In the later 1950s and 1960s the rationale behind the teaching of English as a second language was based on an assimilationist model. Again, the problem was seen to be the pupils themselves. There was a conscious and determined opposition to the Asian child's mother tongue, which was seen as an obstacle to the learning of English. The aim was to teach English quickly so that pupils could 'adjust' into the school system, and 'fit into' society as quickly as possible.

Considerable research evidence made it clear that black pupils were educationally 'underachieving'. Numerous explanations were given. It was argued, for example that black pupils were failing because they experienced 'culture conflict' or 'culture shock'. Many teachers have perpetuated this view, the notion that black people suffer from a lack of 'self-identity'. This view appealed to many white liberals; after all, it was what some members of the Black Movement also seemed to be saying.[23] After a time it began to be stated that black children should be taught an appreciation of their cultural heritage as a way of overcoming their identity crisis. And so 'black studies' were initiated.

There were several difficulties with such projects: faced with the choice of black studies or something so obviously useful as car mechanics, black pupils invariably chose the latter.

Second, black studies were racially divisive, there was a danger of segregation, of associating certain types of pupils with certain types of knowledge. If black pupils were taught 'black studies' as a separate, distinct subject, apart from the white culture, could this not be a form of 'apartheid'? Third, though black studies may have helped raise the consciousness of some groups, they rarely challenged dominant white patterns of thought and control. I contend that the view that black people lack 'self-identity' is false. Young black people know exactly who they are, they have a perceptive understanding of their identities and of the social and political situation.

Another common explanation was in terms of cultural deprivation: black children's primary socialization and pre-school experience was unsatisfactory, the black mother was inadequate, or there was a linguistic deficit. It was usually assumed that 'verbally deprived' children were also 'culturally deprived' — this was the most common explanation of working-class and black underachievement. The remedy for cultural deprivation took the form of compensatory education; positive discrimination was urged — but never practised.

The fact is that black children, growing up in racist societies such as Britain, experience prejudice and discrimination at a very early age. Within the educational system there are specific structures which serve to reproduce educational disadvantage in black pupils. Such mechanisms include testing and grading procedures, practices such as streaming, banding, zoning, and dispersal, wrong placement in special immigrant classes and in schools for the educationally subnormal. There is a denial and devaluation of the black child's culture and language in the curriculum and in the school.

The curriculum and teachers' attitudes

I shall now make a few remarks on two of the mechanisms of racial discrimination: the curriculum and the practices of teachers.

The curriculum, as we know it, has traditions stemming from beyond the Renaissance to the Greeks. But we now take it so much for granted that we no longer examine the assumptions on which the curriculum is based. 3½ per cent of the population is from the black commonwealth and the Asian subcontinent; this constitutes a multicultural, multiethnic society, but this is not reflected, as yet, in the curriculum.[24]

Stereotypes of black people have entered and are passed on through the 'hidden curriculum'. This is particularly noticeable in the text books of African history where images are presented of black people as being uncultured and uncivilized, whilst it is assumed that whites are more intelligent than black people. In short, we undervalue black history, black culture.

Changes are urgently needed not only in the curriculum, but also in the practices of teachers. A significant number of teachers are racist, that is to say they do their jobs in a way that excludes blacks in the classroom. The teachers themselves often have prejudiced stereotypes; they too readily assume that problem children in schools are black. Black kids are thought of as troublesome, stupid, educationally subnormal and these expectations often act as a self-fulfilling prophecy.

One of the best known cases of discrimination is the fact that most black children are put in the lowest streams and are over-represented in special schools. For example, in 1971 immigrants formed 6.5 per cent of all pupils in educationally subnormal schools. The significance of this process has been described by Bernard Coard in his book, *How the West Indian Child is made Educationally Sub-Normal in the British School System*:[25]

> Thus the one way to ensure no changes in the social hierarchy and abundant unskilled labour is to adapt the educational system to meet the needs of the situations to prepare our children for the society's future unskilled and ill-paid jobs. It is in this perspective that we can come to appreciate why so many of our black children are being dumped in the E.S.N. schools, secondary moderns, the lowest streams of the comprehensive schools and 'bussed' and 'banded' about the school system.

There are also some teachers who tend to say that the expectations of black children must not be too high, 'pupils must learn to be realistic'. This too lowers expectations and performance. A black teacher, looking back on his own schooling, remarked:[26]

> The way the teachers cued classes was unfair. They would ask questions to all the white kids who they knew knew the answers. We were always ignored at the back of the class. You would think of

yourself: 'I haven't got much say here, this experience isn't mine.' . . . You began to see the world through a white kid like Janet or John. You were an observer, yet somehow you were also expected to participate. And when you didn't want to join in, you were penalized and that justified them putting you at the back in the first place.

The multicultural model

In recent years the cultural deprivation model has been strongly criticized and though it is still widely held by many administrators and social workers, it has been partly replaced by a new one. In the new model it is assumed that black children fail because of their low self-esteem which is derived from negative white attitudes.[27] The solution to this problem, then, is to boost the low self-image of black children, to give them more self-esteem and, at the same time, to change the attitudes of white teachers and pupils.

The initial strategy, which was based on an assimilationist model, is now changing towards a model of linguistic and cultural pluralism. There is now an increasing acceptance of the new approach which stresses the child's linguistic competencies, and proposes the promotion of the mother tongue/dialect in schools. To say this in another way: the ideology of 'cultural deprivation' has been gradually replaced by a theory of 'linguistic difference'. Creole, for example, is seen as being different rather than a deficit. It is argued that if 'the problem' is one of low black self-esteem, and language is an integral part of identity, the promotion of mother-tongue teaching should increase self-esteem and change attitudes. And so we now find many linguists and educationalists are recommending the promotion of the mother tongue and bi-dialectalism in schools.

The educational 'solution', then, is a cultural one of changing attitudes and promoting 'inter-ethnic respect'. The main strategy now being employed is that of changing the *content* of the curriculum, of replacing the monoethnic, ethnocentric curriculum with a multicultural one. This kind of approach has led to a stress on multiculturalism (the focusing on the lifestyle and beliefs of minority groups); the dissemination of information to counteract racialist myths; and the demolition of racialist stereotypes in books and teaching materials.

Now, I believe that this approach has something to be said for it. It is not wrong — it may even do some good. But it is not enough. Although this new model of multicultural education represents a departure from the increasingly discredited model, it still operates with an inadequate conception of 'what the problem is', and this misconception is reflected in the work done in schools. Why is this model inadequate in combating racism?

First, this model reduces racism to the *attitudes of individuals*, and in doing so fails to locate those attitudes in their economic and political context. In focusing on the indigenous racialism of individuals, this view sees racism as being caused by fear, ignorance, and lack of cultural understanding. Consequently, the aim becomes one of changing the attitudes of white people, thereby establishing a 'pluralistic and tolerant multiracial society'. Although this concern with changing attitudes is a genuine one, there is often a failure to consider and confront the conditions of society that give rise to these attitudes.

At a time when indigenous racism has become a political issue, it is still assumed that it is possible to be politically neutral about race. And so, there are still many schools that fail to relate the racism of the wider society to the racism within schools. Moreover, there are still many teachers who believe that racialism among children does not exist, or, if it does exist, it is only held by a small deviant minority. Similarly, the indigenous racism of teachers and schools is persistently denied. Teachers' unions, for example, fail to question their own racism, and the practices of their members at the workplace. Furthermore, most educational authorities seem to have a policy not to have a policy on race relations.

It is precisely because the problem is seen in an individualistic, 'cultural' way concerning people's attitudes that certain key issues are ignored in 'multicultural' education: the structural racism of schools and institutionalized *state* racism. Issues such as immigration, the location and function of blacks in the economy, black unemployment are never discussed. It is not surprising that black underachievement continues to be a problem. There is still a concern with changing white attitudes, boosting the 'fragile self-esteem' of black pupils, and 'multiculturalizing' the curriculum.

But the problem is *not* of assimilating or integrating newcomers, and the solution is not of overcoming the 'natural handicap' of being non-English, or of 'changing the attitudes' of the indigenous population. As the current 'multicultural' educational model operates with an inadequate economic and political analysis of what racism is, the strategies it adopts are also found to be wanting.

I began this section on discrimination in education with an outline of some of the features of the 'assimilationist' model which was applied to the first generation of immigrants. To understand fully the views of this generation of immigrants on education, one has to appreciate the fact that they were representatives of Britain's colonial heritage. They regarded education as if it was a stepping-stone towards a better life. They believed in educational opportunity, the notion that a good education provides the opportunity of social mobility, of bettering oneself. But as this is a myth, it is not surprising that so many black children did not achieve 'success'.

Since the 1960s the educational model has changed to a multicultural one, but the consciousness of young black people has also changed.[28] They are very different from the first generation; they are much more sceptical and realize that the state does not just bestow 'education'. They know that schooling has certain functions besides child-minding: to develop certain (limited) skills, to hierarchically grade the workforce, and to discipline it. Moreover, they know that schools can do little to change their oppression and exploitation, the position of structural subordination in British society. Racism is not simply the discriminatory attitudes of people with whom blacks come into contact, but rather a specific mechanism which reproduces the black labour force from one generation to another in places and positions that are race-specific. In other words, blacks experience a form of indigenous racism which has its roots in the real material conditions of existence.[29] Such material conditions cannot be simply 'educated' away. Blacks, realizing all this, are becoming a dynamic politicized force and making their views known: 'We're no longer immigrants but Black British, and no power, whether by inducement, coercion or even the most extreme violence will deny us the right to enjoy full and equal British citizenship.'[30]

Chapter 9

Summary and conclusions

From caring to controlling

Let me now summarize the main argument. I began by describing the context in which 'the Great Debate' on education took place in order to show the extensive growth of right-wing ideas in recent years.[1] I mentioned, for example, the 'Black Papers' which contributed to the reactionary framework within which the debate on the purposes of education was conducted. I went on to describe some of the main features of the current crisis in education: the problematic nature of progressivism; the historical origins of discipline and the idea that education has, largely, a disciplinary function; the changes in the labour process and the nature of work that are taking place.

I argued that all aspects of progressivism are being attacked, and that there is a move towards the enforcement of stricter discipline in schools *and* society. An anxiety about the attitudes of the young unemployed is leading to an emphasis on work socialization and there is also an increase of ideological pressures on all who work in educational institutions.[2] In brief, there is a shift in emphasis from 'care' to 'control'.

It was argued that the above features of the crisis, though *real* are but surface appearances. Underlying the appearances – the purpose of a Marxist analysis is to reveal the underlying reality beneath the outer manifestations – there is the reality of a crisis in capitalism. Discussions about education, therefore, can be understood only when related to the economic crisis and the present conjuncture in which the state is playing an increasingly interventionist role. It was suggested, therefore, that we need to examine the relationship between schooling and the state. The origins of the state provision of education were discussed, the liberal view of education and the state being contrasted with some socialist approaches to education.

It was pointed out that the distinguishing feature of state monopoly capitalism is the state's predominance in economic reproduction. As this stage is associated with the growth of expenditure, the development of the welfare state, and the rise of social democratic reformism, these were some of the topics also examined. The assumptions of social democracy — its deep belief in the neutrality of the state and in parliamentarianism — were challenged.[3]

In subsequent chapters differing conceptions of the state were examined and some recent developments in the theory of the state were discussed in order to comprehend how the illusion of the neutral state has been maintained and the political struggle of the working class contained.[4] It was noted that the state was changing its role; it is being forced to become increasingly interventionist in order to secure certain conditions of existence for capitalism. The primary purpose of state intervention is to ensure the social reproduction necessary for class domination.

The conditions of existence of capitalism

It was emphasized that the crisis must be seen in terms of a crisis of capital and that the source of the crisis lies within the contradictions of the capitalist system itself.[5] And so, in Chapters 5 and 6, I described how capitalism introduces more and more mechanization and technology which increases the productivity of labour. As productivity increases, fewer workers are employed by a given amount of capital. The reserve army of labour, the unemployed, increases. There is a tendency for the rate of profit to fall. A fall in the rate of profit forces capitalism to increase the rate of exploitation. Capitalism tries, first, to reduce wages below the value of labour power, and second, to discipline the working class by the intensification of labour.

The crisis, then, is an expression of the contradictions of capitalism. The growth of the state's role, of the state apparatuses and state expenditure follows from these contradictions. Inflation and unemployment increase together. The state intervenes to prevent unemployment. State expenditure must grow or unemployment will grow; state expenditure postpones the immediate consequences of the fall in the rate of profit.

Capitalism attempts to establish the conditions for a higher rate of profit; besides the attempt to force down wages of the working class, capital, itself, has to be re-structured. This means the destruction of less efficient capitals (in a sense a capitalist crisis is a disease *and* a cure), and more centralization of capital. There is then an attack by the capitalist class on state expenditure (education, health, etc. cost money from surplus labour which means less money for accumulation), and a campaign against 'unproductive' workers, most of whom work in the state sector, in an attempt to create a rift within the working class.

The educational crisis, then, is not specific; it is constituted by the general crisis of production. The intervention of the bourgeois state arises directly from the needs of capital, the state intervenes to preserve the conditions of existence of capitalism. It has been argued that the state is attempting to restructure education as part of a wider attempt to maintain control at a time of economic crisis. Education is one state apparatus amongst many attempting to discipline the working class.

Now, education is one of the main sectors concerned with the reproduction of labour power; it provides services in a certain form, in certain relations, and these have to be continually reproduced. The educational system, on the whole, relates its activities to the quantity and quality of the labour force required by the capitalist labour process. In other words, the 'conditions of existence' of capitalism that education fulfils are the production and reproduction of mental and manual labour.

In the context of an economic crisis there is an expulsion of living labour into the ranks of the reserve army which increases working-class militancy. The bourgeoisie mounts a counter-offensive and the state acts to form the political unity of the bourgeoisie. There are cuts in the expenditure on health, education and other welfare services; ideological pressures increase on schools and colleges. Discipline is tightened; control through a wide variety of agencies becomes more coercive. The crisis in education can only be understood in the context of state intervention. The current controversies in education – the attack on progressivism, the stress on work-socialization in the new agencies and training programmes, the centralization of power, the more assertive role of the Department of Education and Science and its closer supervision of the education service and the curriculum – are all symptomatic of an attempt to mobilize counter-tendencies, to restructure capital relations.

Restructuring

The contradictions within capitalism lead to tendencies which require capital (increasingly through state intervention) continually to restructure its own relations of production. Cuts in public expenditure become necessary because state financing reduces the amount of money available for accumulation and profits and this inevitably intensifies the crisis. But, as I remarked, restructuring involves much

111

more than expenditure cutting — transfers in expenditure and reorganization in the interests of greater control are equally important.[6] The 'cuts' are made in such a way that expenditure is as functional as possible for capital. This is why there is an attempt to 'improve' the fit between schools and industry, to make education 'economically relevant'. The economic crisis and the social policies which the Right develop in response to it, also necessitate substantial increases in social control. And so restructuring also includes attempts to improve methods of controlling 'disruptive' and 'delinquent' youth. The increase in deviancy and conflict demands increased expenditures on deviancy control, on police and prisons in the interests of 'law and order'. This is the context in which institutionalized racism, state racism, is being practised; the increased demand for housing, hospitals, transport, education (services which are always deteriorating), can be set in a context of scapegoating blacks.

There is a sense in which the crisis is not only an economic crisis but a crisis of social relations. And so, besides the shift of capital towards the more profitable sectors, and the cuts in public expenditure, there has been a concerted effort to 'manage' the crisis ideologically. It was stated that an increasing centralization and concentration of power is taking place, and that this is related to a shift to the Right.[7] Indeed, it is my view that the features and tendencies I have described in education are manifestations of, and a response to, a right-wing offensive.

The radical Right has effectively intervened in the political spaces, the 'gaps' neglected by the Left. This shift was made possible by a highly successful orchestration of negative feelings about 'the permissive society', the numbers of blacks, the need for 'law and order, and the bureauractic oppressiveness of many welfare state agencies. In other words, the Right successfully mobilized an authoritarian populism at a time of capitalist crisis.[8] A *new* conservative ideology based on a very broad movement has arisen. Supporting 'self-help' and private enterprise, it is nationalist and anti-collectivist; it has specific policies concerning the law, unions, the health service, and the education system. Besides the attack on black workers and their communities, there is an attack on the position of women.[9] An ideological ethos has been created which justifies the removal of women from social production back to the home. At the same time there is an exertion of greater managerial control of the labour process and an attack on the trade unions. In all these respects Thatcherism is a continuation, an intensification, of processes begun by the Labour government.

The same processes can also be seen on the terrain of education. The educational system, too, is being attacked; the government, the media, and industry are focusing on the shortcomings of teachers and schools. It is being said that teachers are failing to give instruction in the basic skills, they are failing to prepare young people for work; furthermore, the school curriculum is irrelevant to the needs of an advanced industrial society. Many parents have felt this too and so these criticisms were readily exploited. After all, much of education, its structure, organization, and practice has been elitist. This could be said about the welfare state in general which embodies a social democratic, Fabian outlook. A characteristic of this outlook, and its expression in terms of social policy, is its reliance on 'experts'. On the basis of 'facts' which they have collected, 'experts' have made the decisions about the forms and content of education.

In other words, the working class itself has not been involved in the decision-making process, but has been acted upon; 'good' has been done to them. And so, when the radical Right made criticisms of a remote bureaucracy, this resonated with many working-class people who experienced many aspects of the welfare state as repressive.[10] It is not surprising that there are ambivalent feelings about schools as there is a real contradiction in that schools are both oppressive *and* potentially liberating.

The radical Right stresses the maintenance of certain unproblematic standards, but the interest in 'standards' is largely rhetorical, a device to gain mass support. The 'new authoritarians' of the Right are not really concerned with standards but with the exercise of *control*. Their demand is that education should become much more 'relevant', that schools should service the technicist needs of industry, and that there must be conformity and control in education as in the work process. And so the ideal of equality of opportunity remains unfulfilled — but now even this 'principle' is being eroded. The main objective of government policies now is to restructure the educational system; this is being done by halting the movement towards comprehensive education, by downgrading the public sector in education, starving it of resources, and shifting resources to the private, independent, sector.[11] With the cuts in state expenditure, the reduction in the teaching force, the worsening of pupil-teacher ratios, the class bias of the education system is getting even wider.

It is now being explicitly stated that education should deliberately and selectively prepare the workforce of the future. What this means in effect, is the induction of the majority of people into routine, standardized alienated labour for the factory and/or the home. Of course, this does not mean that all schools simply function for capital. There are many complex, uneven and contradictory elements that act against and interrupt this reproduction. That is to say, the schools not only reproduce the social relations of production, they also reproduce forms of *resistance*. Many pupils develop a characteristic resistance to the overt aims of schooling; teachers, also, struggle within their workplaces.

Such a view constitutes a break with the determinism of Althusserian theory, which stressed the notion that the state is a repressive state apparatus in which state workers, such as teachers, could do nothing.[12] Though Althusser made the important distinction between state power and state apparatus and argued that the proletariat must seize power in order to destroy the existing bourgeois state apparatus, he neglected the existence of contradictions in and between state apparatuses, the spaces in which state workers can struggle in and against the state.[13]

The issue of resistance brings us to wider questions: How do we construct an opposition to capitalist schooling? At a time when the welfare state is being dismantled, what forms of struggle should we, teachers and students, engage in? I suggest that, first, teachers should begin thinking, collectively, about the politics of learning and teaching. A great deal of work needs to be undertaken by the Left on what a socialist education would consist of, and it needs to be remembered that the education we devise should not be just different in content from orthodox schooling, but be based on different principles.

There will have to be an attempt to involve everyone in a form of politics concerned with the democratization of educational institutions and practices.[14] An attempt must be made to build on the diverse initiatives of different groups of people; women's groups, black organizations, tenant associations, trades councils, shop stewards committees, socialist centres and bookshops, local action committees. Alliances will have to be made linking as many of these diverse extra parliamentary movements as possible.

But practical politics at the local level is not enough. Besides struggle at the grass roots, links must be made between community politics and national politics. There are so many divisions to overcome — the divisions between whites and blacks, men and women, employed and unemployed — that revolutionary political organizations are essential to counteract fragmentation and to orchestrate different campaigns in and against the state.

What do you think?

Notes

1 The attack on progressive education

1 Societies are subject to periods of 'moral panic' when the official reaction to persons or series of events, is out of all proportion to the actual threat offered. For an incisive account of the way in which the newspapers dealt with the subjects of education, young people and schools during the summer of 1977 see *Lunatic Ideas*, Corner House Bookshop, 14 Endell Street, London W.C.2.

2 Brian Simon, 'Education and the Right offensive', *Marxism Today*, February, 1980, p. 13. See also 'Contemporary problems in educational theory', in Brian Simon, *Intelligence, Psychology and Education*, London, Lawrence & Wishart, 1979.

3 Samuel Bowles and Herbert Gintis, *Schooling in Capitalist America*, London, Routledge & Kegan Paul, 1976, p. 44.

4 Rachel Sharp and Anthony Green, *Education and Social Control: a Study in Progressive Primary Education*, London, Routledge & Kegan Paul, 1975.

5 Ibid., p. 218-21.

6 Ibid., p. 222.

7 Ibid., p. 224.

8 Some of the assumptions of progressive pedagogy are also examined in Basil Bernstein, 'Class and pedagogies: visible and invisible', in *Class, Codes and Control*, vol. 3, London, Routledge & Kegan Paul, 1975. He suggests that in progressive teaching the control of the teacher is implicit rather than explicit and the criteria for evaluating the pedagogy are multiple and diffuse, and so not easily measured. The teachers' pedagogical theory of play and the theories of Freud, Piaget, or Chomsky are invisible and so implicit to the child. The theory gives rise to a total — but invisible — surveillance. For Bernstein, progressivism had its origins in the rise of the new middle class.

9 Gramsci's work is highly relevant though his notes on education are inconclusive. His emphasis on discipline, and even coercion in

the early years at school in subjects like Latin and 'the instrumental notions of schooling — reading, writing, sums, geography,
and history', explain why he has sometimes been seen as being
against progressivism. He stressed the teachers' dogmatic role and
the inculcation of good work habits especially in the first stages
of school. In his view, the curriculum of the school was important
also, and his curriculum proposals appear to contain many traditional and conservative elements. His 'conservatism', however,
should be seen in the context of his insistence on the production
through education of a class and its elite, working-class intellectuals, who will work towards the establishment of a counter-
hegemony. See Quintin Hoare and Geoffrey Nowell-Smith (eds),
Antonio Gramsci, *Selections from the Prison Notebooks*, London,
Lawrence & Wishart, 1971, pp. 24-43; Harold Entwistle, *Antonio
Gramsci: Conservative Schooling for Radical Politics*, London,
Routledge & Kegan Paul, 1979.

10 Neville Bennett, *Teaching Styles and Pupil Progress*, London,
Open Books, 1976.

11 Dave Harris and John Holmes, 'Open-ness and control in higher
education: towards a critique of the Open University', in Roger
Dale, Geoff Esland and Madeleine MacDonald (eds), *Schooling
and Capitalism: a Sociological Reader*, London, Routledge &
Kegan Paul, 1976.

12 Ralph Turner, 'Sponsored and contest mobility and the school
system', in Earl Hopper (ed.), *Readings in the Theory of Educational Systems*, London, Hutchinson, 1971, p. 74.

13 This is, of course, not to deny its many achievements. It has, for
example, awarded degrees to over 30,000 students in eleven years.
The contradiction remains: though founded by Harold Wilson
and Jennie Lee to provide second-chance education, there is a
middle-class bias of applications. But Conservatives remain sceptical of the institution in spite of the fact that each degree course
costs less at the Open University than anywhere else.

14 That, thirty years after the welfare state, no significant reductions
in class inequalities have been achieved has been shown by A.H.
Halsey *et al.*, *Origins and Destinations: Family, Class and Education in Modern Britain*, Oxford, Clarendon Press, 1980.

15 David Hargreaves, *Social Relations in a Secondary School*, London,
Routledge & Kegan Paul, 1967.

16 See Sara Delamont, *Interaction in the Classroom*, London,
Methuen, 1976; Michael Stubbs, *Language, Schools and Classrooms*, London, Methuen, 1976.

17 For a discussion of the issues raised in this paragraph see Madan
Sarup, *Marxism and Education*, London, Routledge & Kegan
Paul, 1978, pp. 85-103.

18 But John White objects: 'Too much freedom to do what he or she
wants is not going to help the child whose desires and abilities are
very limited to acquire new ones ... Children will tend to be

imprisoned within a way of life with which they are already familiar.' He believes that socialist education should not be identified with extreme 'progressivism'; that the extreme libertarianism of some child-centred education has nothing to do with socialism. See John White, 'Socialist perspectives on the curriculum', in David Rubinstein (ed.), *Education and Equality*, Penguin, 1979.

19 Bourdieu is interested in the ideology of culture, power, social reproduction and their relation to education. Influenced by Durkheim and Lèvi-Strauss, Bourdieu looks for homologies and *structural* patterns. In his view it is an illusion that education is neutral; the notion that school is a liberating force is a twentieth-century myth. There are cultural struggles in which classes compete for power and dominant groups have access to the power to impose meanings, 'symbolic violence'. Cultural capital, comparable to economic capital, is transmitted by inheritance and invested in order to be cultivated. Cultural privileges become portrayed as natural phenomena; social gifts are presented as if they were individual gifts. For the ruling class there is *more* power and privilege whilst for the working class there is domestication. Thus the system 'confers on the privileged the supreme privilege of not seeing themselves as privileged [and] manages the more easily to convince the disinherited that they owe their scholastic and social destiny to their lack of gifts or merits, because in matters of culture absolute dispossession excludes awareness of being dispossessed.' For a systematic exposition of how power is maintained by the transmission of cultural capital see Pierre Bourdieu and Jean Claude Passeron, *Reproduction in Education, Society and Culture*, London, Sage, 1977.

20 Raymond Williams, 'Base and superstructure in Marxist cultural theory', in Dale, Esland and Macdonald, op. cit., p. 206.

21 As this is the only aspect of progressivism on which Willis's book focuses, I assume he is against it. It should be noted that his argument could be extended; just as many schools have replaced coercion by an emphasis on gaining consent by the taught, similarly many states in Western Europe have attempted to incorporate the working class by developing social welfare policies. Paul Willis, *Learning to Labour*, London, Saxon House, 1977, p. 83.

22 Ibid., p. 178.

23 Ibid., p. 128.

2 The enforcement of discipline

1 Michel Foucault, *Discipline and Punish*, Penguin, 1977. There are useful articles on Foucault in *Radical Philosophy*, no. 16, spring 1977 and no. 17, summer 1977.

2 Foucault, op. cit., p. 150.

3 Ibid., p. 166.

4 Ibid., p. 157.
5 Ibid., p. 172.
6 Ibid., p. 178.
7 Ibid., p. 146.
8 Ibid., p. 192.
9 Ibid., p. 200.
10 Ibid., p. 27.
11 Ibid., p. 304.
12 The essential point that for Marx and Lenin revolution is not only about the destruction of the bourgeois state as a power separate from and counterposed to the masses, but also about replacement by a power of a new type, is forcefully argued in 'Lenin's *State and Revolution*', in Lucio Colletti, *From Rousseau to Lenin*, London, New Left Books, 1979, p. 219.
13 Foucault, op. cit., p. 26.
14 See Bob Fine, 'Struggles against discipline: the theory and politics of Michel Foucault', in *Capital and Class*, 9, autumn 1979, p. 92.
15 Foucault, op. cit., p. 307.
16 For an elaboration of these points about how pupils labour and its product, knowledge, is reduced to the status of a commodity, see Ian Hextall and Madan Sarup, 'School knowledge, evaluation and alienation', in Michael Young and Geoff Whitty (eds), *Society, State and Schooling*, Ringmer, Lewes, Falmer Press, 1977, p. 155.
17 Ibid., p. 73. It has been argued that Althusser's work can be read as a functionalist account; see, for example, Michael Erben and Denis Gleeson, 'Education as reproduction', in Young and Whitty, op. cit.

3 The emphasis on work-socialization

1 'A group of MPs, most of them Tories, have warned the Government that public disorder could break out in Wales, if it does not take immediate action to relieve unemployment believed to be near 20 per cent', the *Guardian*, Friday 1 August 1980. 'Mr Stan. Newens (Labour, Harlow) warned that Mrs Thatcher's policies could lead to "social unrest". Unemployment had led to the outbreak of fascism and other extremist creeds in other parts of the world' (the *Guardian*, Friday 25 July 1980).
2 Simon Frith, *The Sociology of Rock*, London, Constable, 1976. See also Dick Hebdige, *Subculture: the Meaning of Style*, London, Methuen, 1979.
3 Against the views of Coleman, Jencks, and others it has been argued by Rutter *et al.*, that children's behaviour and attitudes *are* shaped and influenced by their experiences at school and, in particular, by the qualities of the school as a social institution. See Michael Rutter, Barbara Maughan, Peter Mortimore and Janet Ouston, *Fifteen Thousand Hours: Secondary Schools and their*

Effects on Children, London Open Books, 1979. For a critique of the above research, see Trevor Pateman, *Can Schools Educate?* (1980), Jean Stroud Publisher, PO Box 12, Lewes, East Sussex BN7 1AZ.

4 Doing nothing does not deserve to be neglected as an activity. See Paul Corrigan, *Schooling the Smash Street Kids*, London, Macmillan, 1979, p. 126.

5 It has been proposed by the government that in the national interest all children in secondary schools should compulsorily study, till they are 16, a core of five subjects: maths, English, science, religious education, and a foreign language. The government's view of what is in the national interest is based on the needs of manufacturing industry for recruits with certain basic skills. A core-curriculum such as this would further reinforce the process that is already occurring – the gradual redefinition of 'education'. Ironically, such a narrow curriculum – with *no* history, geography, social sciences and politics, music and art – would be of little use to young people facing a future of 'enforced leisure'.

6 The Manpower Services Commission is increasingly involved with the growing army of the young unemployed. It is an organization directly responsible to the Secretary of State for Employment and is organized regionally by technocrats. In 1978 it received fifty million pounds to implement school/work policies. The MSC provides two-thirds of its training in educational institutions, such as Further Education Colleges, which it pays to put on courses for it. Recently it has been suggested that all young people between 16 and 18 be given a weekly 'training for work' allowance (i.e. a subsistence wage plus pocket money, as in the Federal German Republic).

7 Harry Braverman, *Labour and Monopoly Capital*, New York, Monthly Review Press.

8 For a useful discussion on the office and the impact of microelectronics see Jane Barker and Hazel Downing, 'Word processing and the transformation of the patriarchal relations of control in the office', *Capital and Class*, 10, spring 1980.

9 These managerial strategies are fully discussed by Andrew L. Friedman, *Industry and Labour*, London Macmillan, 1977, Chapters 6 and 7.

10 It has been argued that the Bolsheviks took over from the Second International the notion that Western societies were the only model for the building of socialist society. Lenin wished to adopt the large-scale industry of Western countries, to catch up and surpass them. He argued (as did Trotsky) that there was no need to invent some original way of organizing labour as capitalism had created and perfected one that was immediately usable. Lenin introduced Taylorism without examining its inherently alienating character. He did not realize that the stress on absolute subordination in production, and to the Party, contained the danger of

influencing the general character of the new society at every level. For this argument see, for example, Carmen Claudin-Urondo, *Lenin and the Cultural Revolution*, Brighton, Harvester Press, 1977.

11 The work of Baran and Sweezy, who attempted to 'revise' Marx's economic theory, powerfully but implicitly structures Braverman's whole analysis. For an elaboration of the criticisms in this section and a most useful bibliography see Tony Elger, 'Valorization and deskilling: a critique of Braverman', in *Capital and Class*, 7, spring 1979.

12 For a seminal discussion of scientific management and Taylorism see Alfred Sohn-Rethel, *Intellectual and Manual Labour*, London, Macmillan, 1978, pp. 140-72.

13 Paul Willis, 'Shop-floor culture, masculinity and the wage form', in John Clarke, Chas Critcher and Richard Johnson (eds), *Working Class Culture: Studies in History and Theory*, London, Hutchinson, 1979. An earlier version of this paper, 'The class significance of school counter-culture', appears in Martyn Hammersley and Peter Woods (eds), *The Process of Schooling*, London, Routledge & Kegan Paul, 1976.

14 Paul Willis, *Learning to Labour*, Farnborough, Saxon House, 1977.

15 Ibid., p. 150.

16 Ibid., p. 130.

17 Ibid., p. 189.

18 Q. Hoare and G. Nowell-Smith (eds), *Antonio Gramsci, Selections from the Prison Notebooks*, London, Lawrence & Wishart, 1971.

19 The commitment of European education systems, by and large, to literacy as a primary skill reveals a presupposition of immense proportions. Writing and reading are not the 'natural' processes that liberal humanism presupposes; they mask a complex political and economic ideology. Indeed, Philippe Sollers has suggested that in a society which has imposed and institutionalized the written form of language as an overall dominating feature of its way of life, all writing is political writing: 'Writing is the continuation of politics by other means.' It has been said that mass literacy, and an educational system firmly based on it, has tended in twentieth-century Europe and America to establish and reinforce an equation between literature and life that would have astonished any preceding age. When that mediation comes through the mediation of literary criticism, to acquire positive prescriptive force in respect of morality, politics, even economics, and when its presuppositions find themselves transmitted at large and unquestioned throughout an all-embracing system of education, then it seems reasonable to expect that 'crises' in one area will find themselves mirrored in another. See Terence Hawkes, *Structuralism and Semiotics*, London, Methuen, 1977, p. 156.

20 Willis, op. cit., p. 92.

21 The belief that to become a useful member of society requires the destruction of working class culture and its replacement with

values associated with discipline is not new. In the period from before the Boer War down to the First World War, the heyday of imperialism and nationalism, there was a massive attempt to transform popular ways of life and modes of belief. The law was used for the regulation of leisure pursuits, to remove working-class young people from uncontrolled contexts into more pro-vided, 'organized' leisure forms. Among the organizations for working-class youth there were many paramilitary movements whose members wore uniforms, carried weapons, practised drill and were superintended by ex-army officers. Members of the Boys' Brigade used to carry Martini-Henry Carbines and those of the Church Lads Brigade were taught military drill and shooting. Even the Boy Scouts were more military and militant than its founder, Baden Powell, admitted. The social role of these 'clubs' was the inculcation of discipline and duty. The army served as a mode for both its organization and training goals. The military structure of organized authority by ranks and levels was a structure thought to provide a model for social organization. And patriotism, stimu-lated by the challenge of rapid German economic growth, was linked to perseverance, punctuality and diligence. Boys trained as Scouts, or cadets or in the lads club or Street Boys' Union were all said to be that much more hardworking and useful to their employers. See Michael Blanch, 'Imperialism, nationalism and organized youth', in John Clarke *et al.* (eds), *Working Class Culture*, London, Hutchinson, 1979.

22 As I have drawn so heavily on Braverman's thesis, one of the criticisms that could be made of this chapter is that by over-emphasizing the structural changes caused by the capitalist labour process, I have been guilty of a form of technological determin-ism. I want to deny this charge and argue that changes in the labour process are changes, too, in modes of control of collective labour, and that collective labour is an *ideological* as well as an economic category.

4 Schooling and the state

1 For a discussion of how the Elementary Education Act of 1870 caused hardship to many parents because they lost a valuable supplement to the family income with the introduction of com-pulsory school attendance, see John Hurt, *Elementary Schooling and the Working Classes 1860-1918*, London, Routledge & Kegan Paul, 1979.

2 See Louis Althusser, 'Ideology and ideological state apparatuses', in B.R. Cosin (ed.), *Education: Structure and Society*, Penguin, 1972. p. 258.

3 See, for example, Steven Rose and Hilary Rose, 'The politics of neurobiology: biologism in the service of the state'; Clarence J.

Karier, 'Testing for order and control in the corporate liberal state'; Paul Henderson, 'Class structure and the concept of intelligence', in Roger Dale, *et al.* (eds), *Schooling and Capitalism*, London, Routledge & Kegan Paul, 1976.

4 'In any period it is upon a very small minority that the discerning appreciation of art and literature depends ... upon this minority depends our power of profiting by the finest human experience of the past; they keep alive the subtlest and most perishable parts of tradition. Upon them depend the implicit standards that order the finer living of an age.' F.R. Leavis, quoted in Raymond Williams, *Culture and Society 1780-1950*, Penguin, 1958, p. 247.

5 See Kevin Harris, *Education and Knowledge*, London, Routledge & Kegan Paul, 1979, p. 139.

6 See, for example, the work of Ralph Miliband, *The State in Capitalist Society*, London, Quartet, 1969; J. Urry and J. Wakeford (eds), *Power in Britain*, London, Heinemann, 1973; J. Westergaard and H. Resler, *Class in a Capitalist Society: A Study of Contemporary Britain*, London, Heinemann, 1975.

7 Samuel Bowles and Herbert Gintis, *Schooling in Capitalist America*, London, Routledge & Kegan Paul, 1976.

8 See, for example, the critique in Madan Sarup, *Marxism and Education*, London, Routledge & Kegan Paul, 1978, pp. 165-84.

9 Richard Johnson, ' "Really Useful Knowledge": radical education and working class culture, 1790-1848', in John Clarke, *et al.* (eds), *Working Class Culture*, London, Hutchinson, 1979.

10 Ibid., p. 76.

11 Ibid., p. 100.

12 Ibid., p. 95.

13 Ibid., p. 101.

14 The passionate belief in an independent working-class education can be seen in the life and work of men such as Albert Mansbridge, John Dent, Joseph Wright, Tommy Jackson, Tom McGuire, Keir Hardie, and many others. They were part of a working class culture of autodidacticism. These people had an incredible motivation for book-learning and valued philosophy highly. They read Darwin and Haeckel; they studied Plato, Kant, Hegel, and were inspired by Dietzgen, Marx and Engels. The idea of state education, however, had a tremendous appeal in the late nineteenth century. At this time Thomas Green, a neo-Hegelian philosopher, was arguing against charity and for a compulsory comprehensive educational system. In his view the function of the state was to bring out the 'higher self' of the individual citizen. But the consequences of state education have been complex and contradictory. See, for example, Anne Phillips and Tim Putnam, 'Education for emancipation: the movement for independent working class education 1908-1928', in *Capital and Class*, 10, spring 1980.

5 The increase in state intervention

1 'State intervention in economic life, managed economy, economic programming, indicative planning are not the least bit neutral from the social point of view ... increasingly the state becomes the guarantor of capitalist profit ... In the final analysis, this state guarantee of profits represents a redistribution of the national income in favour of the leading monopolistic groups through the agency of the state' (Ernest Mandel, *An Introduction to Marxist Theory*, London, Pathfinder Press, 1970, p. 76). Other useful books for those beginning the study of Marxist economics include: Ben Fine, *Marx's Capital*, London, Macmillan, 1975; Geoffrey Kay, *Development and Underdevelopment: a Marxist Analysis*, London, Macmillan, 1975; Geoffrey Kay, *The Economic Theory of the Working Class*, London, Macmillan, 1979.

2 David Yaffe, *The State and the Capitalist Crisis*, R.C.G. Publications, 1976, p. 13. Much of what follows is indebted to David Yaffe; see particularly his article 'Inflation, the crisis and the post-war boom', in *Revolutionary Communist*, no. 3/4, November 1975.

3 See the useful selection of recent articles edited by Theo Nichols, *Capital and Labour: Studies in the Capitalist Labour Process*, London, Fontana, 1980.

4 See Tom Nairn, 'Anatomy of the Labour Party', in Perry Anderson and Robin Blackburn (eds), *Towards Socialism*, London, Merlin, 1967.

5 For an elaboration of these points see Dan Finn, Neil Grant, Richard Johnson, 'Social democracy, education and the crisis', in Centre for Contemporary Cultural Studies, *On Ideology*, London, Hutchinson, 1978.

6 E.P. Thompson, *Whigs and Hunters*, Penguin, 1975, p. 264. For an assessment of Thompson's work, see Perry Anderson, *Arguments Within English Marxism*, London, New Left Books, 1980.

7 Pashukanis believed that law was a bourgeois form of control/regulation and had become an independent force (above society) with its own mechanisms. The law had the appearance of equality when in reality there was an underlying inequality. In his view, the social foundation of the law was commodity-exchange; as long as there was commodity-exchange there has to be law. He believed that the law was not above society, nor was it a neutral instrument. Critical of the vulgar materialists, who only looked at the content of the law and neglected its form, Pashukanis wanted to bring form and content together. He argued for less and less regulation, and wanted to bring lay people into the legal process. E.B. Pashukanis, *Law and Marxism: a General Theory*, London, Ink Links, 1978.

8 In Gramsci's work the concept of hegemony shifted away from an analysis of the social alliances of the proletariat in Russia towards

an analysis of the structures of bourgeois power in the West. He extended the concept to the study of mechanisms of bourgeois rule over the working class in a stabilized capitalist society. The cultural emphasis that the idea of hegemony acquired also produced a new Marxist theory of intellectuals. See Perry Anderson, 'The antinomies of Antonio Gramsci', *New Left Review*, 100, November 1976-January 1977; C. Boggs, *Gramsci's Marxism*, London, Pluto Press, 1976.

9 The authors argue that the police, courts, press and government over-reacted to muggings in England (1972-3). The incidence of mugging was exaggerated. (It should be noted that statistics often have an ideological function – they appear to ground controversial beliefs in incontrovertible 'facts'.) *The police* were preparing for mugging long before it occurred. Relations between blacks and police were bad and, perhaps, the police even 'caused' mugging to happen. *The courts* also contributed to the shaping of public opinion (through the statements of judges when 'summing-up' cases). The consensus approach in Britain, which affects the structuring of news in *the media* is also fully discussed by the authors. The media are the 'primary definers' of topics, they lay down the issues that are to be discussed, and crystallize public opinion. Stuart Hall *et al.* contend that the press acts as a conveyer of dominant ideology and is used by the powerful to justify their actions. This does not mean that agencies such as the police, courts and media act consciously to create a 'moral panic' (an event which is made to seem more threatening than it is). The agencies, too, are 'acting out a script which they do not write'. In the authors' view, a crisis of hegemony occurs when consensus breaks down and coercion shows through. In Britain the turning point (from consensus to coercion) was 1966. It is in this way that the 'Exceptional State' began to emerge. Stuart Hall, Chas Critcher, Tony Jefferson, John Clarke, Brian Roberts, *Policing the Crisis: Mugging, the State, and Law and Order*, London, Macmillan, 1978.

10 Ibid., p. 321.

6 The growing nexus between state and capital

1 Ben Fine and Lawrence Harris, *Rereading Capital*, London, Macmillan, 1979. It should be pointed out that in opposition to Fine and Harris, some writers, like Poulantzas, assert that periodization into stages cannot be done, it is only social formations that can be periodized, since it is in them that the class struggle is enacted.

2 The term 'labour aristocracy' refers to a section of the proletariat bought by, or at least paid by, the bourgeoisie: 'Imperialism, the partition of the world and the exploitation of other countries . . . which means high monopoly profits for a handful of very rich

countries, creates the economic possibility of bribing the upper strata of the proletariat, and thereby fosters, gives form to, and strengthens opportunism' (V.I. Lenin, *Imperialism, the Highest Stage of Capitalism*, Moscow, Foreign Languages Press, p. 125).

3 Miliband identifies various agencies that are concerned with the legitimation of power (the securing of consent): Conservative parties, churches, nationalism and patriotism, business, communications media, and education. He suggests that, for the vast majority, schools perform a class-confirming role. The fact that some working-class children are upwardly mobile serves to foster the idea that those who are not are deficient. The educational system creates the impression, not least among its victims, that their *social* disadvantages exist because of *personal*, limited innate capacities. Ralph Miliband, *The State in Capitalist Society*, London, Quartet, 1973. For the polemic between Poulantzas and Miliband about the latter's thesis, see Robin Blackburn (ed.), *Ideology in Social Science*, London, Fontana, 1972, pp. 238-62.

4 Nicos Poulantzas, *Political Power and Social Classes*, London, New Left Books, 1973; *Classes in Contemporary Capitalism*, London, New Left Books, 1975.

5 For further criticisms of Poulantzas see Simon Clarke, 'Marxism, sociology and Poulantzas' theory of the state', in *Capital and Class*, 2, summer 1977.

6 See John Holloway and Sol Picciotto (eds), *State and Capital: a Marxist Debate*, London, Edward Arnold, 1978, especially Chapter 1; and their article 'Capital, crisis and the state', in *Capital and Class*, 2, summer 1977, p. 76.

7 This can be done, for example, by the institutionalizing of a particular vision of reality. Roland Barthes has argued that the institutionalizing of a particular series of 'classic' texts and of appropriate 'interpretations' of them in an educational system which processes all the members of the society, can clearly act as a potent 'normalizing' force. All aspects of bourgeois life silently acquire the same air of naturalness, of rightness, of universality and inevitability. Bourgeois *écriture* is not innocent. It does not simply reflect reality, it *shapes* reality in its own image, acting as the institutionalized carrier, the transmitter of the bourgeois way of life and its values. See Roland Barthes, *Writing Degree Zero*, London, Cape, 1967.

7 Women and education

1 Sheila Rowbotham, *Hidden from History*, London, Pluto Press, 1973. For the history of English feminist thought see also: Ray Strachey, *The Cause*, London Virago, 1978; E. Sylvia Pankhurst, *The Suffragette Movement*, London, Longmans, 1931; Jill Liddington and Jill Norris, *One Hand Tied Behind Us*, London, Virago, 1978.

2 See, for example, Rayna Reiter (ed.), *Toward an Anthropology of Women*, New York, Monthly Review Press, 1975 and the journal *Critique of Anthropology*, nos. 9 and 10, Women's Issue, 1977.

3 For a clear and useful discussion of these two positions see Roberta Hamilton, *The Liberation of Women*, London, Allen & Unwin, 1978, Chapter 4.

4 Shulamith Firestone, *The Dialectic of Sex*, New York, Morrow, 1970. For a critique of Firestone see Hilary Rose and Jalna Hanmer, 'Women's Liberation: reproduction and the technological fix', in Hilary Rose and Steven Rose (eds), *The Political Economy of Science*, London, Macmillan, 1976.

5 Zillah Eisenstein (ed.), *Capitalist Patriarchy and the Case for Socialist Feminism*, New York, Monthly Review Press, 1979.

6 See D.H.J. Morgan, *Social Theory and the Family*, London, Routledge & Kegan Paul, 1975, especially the chapters on the politics of the family, women as a social class, sex, and capitalism.

7 For this type of argument see Ann Foreman, *Femininity as Alienation: Women and the Family in Marxism and Psychoanalysis*, London, Pluto Press, 1977.

8 Miriam E. David, 'The family-education couple: towards an analysis of the William Tyndale dispute', in Gary Littlejohn *et al.* (eds), *Power and the State*, London, Croom Helm, 1978, p. 165; Miriam E. David, *The State, the Family and Education*, London, Routledge & Kegan Paul, 1980.

9 Rosemary Deem, *Women and Schooling*, London, Routledge & Kegan Paul, 1978, p. 28.

10 Madeleine MacDonald, Sociocultural Reproduction and Women's Education, in Rosemary Deem (ed.), *Schooling for Women's Work*, London, Routledge & Kegan Paul, 1980. MacDonald suggests that femininity can be both a prison and an escape route — it can be used as a legitimation to turn away from the frustrations of school and meaningless employment. See also Angela McRobbie, 'Working class girls and the culture of femininity', in *Women Take Issue* (Women's Studies Group, Centre for Contemporary Cultural Studies), London, Hutchinson, 1978.

11 Sue Sharpe, *'Just Like a Girl': How Girls Learn to be Women*, Penguin, 1976, p. 148. Chapter 8, which describes the attitudes and experiences of West Indian and Asian girls, is particularly helpful.

12 But schools are slowly changing. The curriculum operates on at least two levels. There is the 'blue-print' level of public statements (such as Education Acts), where there is a commitment to equality and the breaking up of stereotypes. But in contrast there is another level where, because of the socialization of teachers and pupils, what actually occurs in schools is very different from the explicit, 'official' level. The implicit assumptions of three educational reports (the Norwood, Crowther and Newsom Reports) are examined by Ann Marie Wolpe, in 'The official ideology of education

for girls', in Michael Flude and John Ahier, *Educability, Schools and Ideology*, London, Croom Helm, 1977, p. 142. She argues that the secondary school institutionalizes the dominant gender role and that the content of these reports, besides forming guidelines, filter down and become part of the 'common code' of the teachers themselves.

13 Karen Jones, 'Women's Education', Educational Studies, *Education, Economy and Politics*, Block 5, The Open University, 1977.

14 E. Belotti, *Little Girls*, London Writers' and Readers' Publishing Co-operative, 1975.

15 A view that has gathered some adherents recently is the one that emphasizes that womens' oppression takes place largely *at the level of ideology* and that ideology is autonomous. Coward and Ellis argue that Marxism has not been successful in some ways because of the limitations of economism. Following Jacques Lacan, they argue that language is not a tool or an instrument that simply reflects the 'real'. Language is not determined by the mode of production, nor is it determining. Believing that something is missing in Althusser's conceptualization of the different levels of practice, the economic, political and ideological, they have added a fourth: signifying practice. They state that it is not possible to separate ideology from language; ideology is in language. Rosalind Coward and John Ellis, *Language and Materialism*, London, Routledge & Kegan Paul, 1977.

16 These points are discussed in Ann Marie Wolpe, 'Education and the sexual division of labour', in Annette Kuhn and Anne Marie Wolpe (eds), *Feminism and Materialism*, London, Routledge & Kegan Paul, 1978.

17 Olivia Adamson, Carol Brown, Judith Harrison and Judy Price, 'Women's oppression under capitalism', *Revoluntionary Communist* no. 5, 1976.

18 Friedrich Engels, *The Origin of the Family, Private Property and the State*, London, Pathfinder Press, 1972.

19 The literature on the debate is large but recent work includes Veronica Beechey, 'Some notes on female wage labour in capitalist production', *Capital and Class*, 3, 1977. This paper begins with criticisms of the mechanistic form of explanation provided by Engels. Maxine Molyneux, 'Beyond the domestic labour debate', *New Left Review*, no. 116, 1979. Diane Elson, 'The value theory of labour', in Diane Elson (ed.), *Value: the Representation of Labour in Capitalism*, London, CSE Books, 1979.

20 These theories are fully discussed in Veronica Beechey, 'Women and production: a critical analysis of some sociological theories of women's work', in Kuhn and Wolpe, op. cit., p. 168.

21 Absolute surplus value is produced by a lengthening of the working day beyond the number of hours during which the worker produces the value which is only the equivalent of her wages. Relative surplus value is produced by increasing the productivity of labour

in the wage-goods industry sector, which enables the worker to reproduce the equivalent of her wages in a shorter portion of the working day, thereby increasing surplus-value without a lengthening of the working day.

22 Counter Information Services, *Crisis: Women Under Attack*, Anti-Report no. 15, CIS, 9 Poland Street, London W.1.

23 Christine Delphy, *The Main Enemy: a Materialist Analysis of Women's Oppression*, London, Women's Research and Resource Centre Publications, 1977. Though Delphy sees her work as an extension of materialism, her thesis is really a radical subversion of Marxism; for a critique of Delphy, see M. Barrett and M. McIntosh, 'Towards a materialist feminism', in *Feminist Review*, Issue no. 1, January 1979.

24 Heidi Hartmann, 'The unhappy marriage of Marxism and feminism: towards a more progressive union', *Capital and Class*, 8, 1979.

25 An example is Eileen Byrne, *Women and Education*, London, Tavistock, 1978; stemming from a liberal feminist tradition, her work stresses the importance of equal rights. She has a faith that attitudes can be changed and that equal opportunity be realized − but she does not question schooling itself.

26 Mary McIntosh, 'The state and the oppression of women', in Kuhn and Wolpe, op. cit.

27 See, for example, Sheila Rowbotham, Hilary Wainwright and Lynne Segal, *Beyond the Fragments*, London, Merlin, 1979. For further information on the women's movement the reader should consult Women's Research and Resources Centre, 190, Upper Street, London N.1.

8 Race, imperialism and education

1 Though the chapters on women and race are separate these categories are not distinct. Readers will notice many *similarities*, on the economic political and ideological levels which I have not made explicit, between the two oppressed groups. For the study of race relations see Gordon Bowker and John Carrier, *Race and Ethnic Relations: Sociological Readings*, London, Hutchinson, 1976; John Rex, *Race Relations in Sociological Theory*, London, Weidenfeld & Nicolson, 1970; Sami Zubaida, *Race and Racialism*, London, Tavistock, 1970.

2 Stephen Castles and Godula Kosack, *Immigrant Workers and Class Structure in Western Europe*, Oxford University Press, 1973; John Rex and Sally Tomlinson, *Colonial Immigrants in a British City: a Class Analysis*, London, Routledge & Kegan Paul, 1979.

3 A. Sivandan, 'Race, class and the state: the black experience in Britain', *Race and Class*, 17, no. 4, 1976; this is also a pamphlet obtainable from the Institute of Race Relations, 247 Pentonville Road, London N1 9NG. *Crisis: Racism − Who Profits*, Counter-

Information Services, Anti-Report no. 16, available from CIS, 9 Poland Street, London W.1.

4 V.I. Lenin, *Imperialism, the Highest Stage of Capitalism*, Peking, Foreign Language Press, 1975.

5 Ibid., p. 73.

6 These terms are Gunder Frank's; his theory is that underdevelopment is produced and increasingly reproduced by the development of the advanced capitalist nations. This development destroys the precapitalist industries in the Third World, draws those nations into the capitalist market and, by appropriating surplus from them, prevents them from accumulating capital. See André Gunder Frank, *Capitalism and Underdevelopment in Latin America*, New York, Monthly Review Press, 1969. In a trenchant critique of Frank's thesis, Laclau has argued that the economy of a peasant village (in Latin America for instance) may be non-capitalist, even if production is ultimately for the capitalist market. There are still social formations which do not have specifically capitalist relations of production. Second, Frank's view that the dominated countries are capitalist, with capitalist relations of production, fails to distinguish between a mode of production and a social formation. The dominated countries are social formations, the product of an articulation of different modes of production. Moreover, Frank's thesis that surplus is appropriated by capitals in the advanced capitalist countries is not sufficient to demonstrate that the backwardness of the rest of the world is thereby increased. Indeed, it could be argued that the expansion of capital has been responsible for a development in the manufacturing sector of the third world economies. See Ernesto Laclau, 'Feudalism and capitalism in Latin America', in *Politics and Ideology in Marxist Theory*, London, New Left Books, 1977. For the experience of migrant workers in the metropolitan centres, see John Berger and Jean Mohr, *A Seventh Man*, Penguin, 1975.

7 Evidence for these statements is presented in 'Racism, imperialism, and the working class', *Revolutionary Communist*, no. 9. I wish to acknowledge a debt to this carefully reasoned analysis.

8 See Karl Marx, *Capital*, vol. 1, Penguin, 1976, Chapter 15.

9 See, for example, Jorge Lorrain, *The Concept of Ideology*, London, Hutchinson, 1979; Paul Hirst, *On Law and Ideology*, London, Macmillan, 1979.

10 'What is believed to be essential for mental health is that the infant and young child should experience a warm, intimate and continuous relationship with his mother (or permanent mother-substitute) in which both find satisfaction and enjoyment' (John Bowlby, *Child Care and the Growth of Love*, Penguin, 2nd edn, 1965, p. 13). See *Attachment and Loss*, 3 vols, Penguin, 1971, 1975 and 1979. Much of Bowlby's work emphasizes the ill effects of maternal deprivation, a theme which has been taken up by many others. It has been suggested, for example, that 'adequate financial reward

should be provided so that no mother of children under five has to go to work for financial reasons'. See Doria Pilling and Mia Kellmer Pringle, *Controversial Issues in Child Development*, London, Paul Elek, 1978, p. 6.

11 For the assumptions behind British family policy and its consequences see, for example, the work of Hilary Land, *The Family, the State and the Labour Market*, London, Martin Robertson, 1980.

12 Steven Rose, 'Scientific racism and ideology: the IQ racket from Galton and Jensen', in S. Rose and H. Rose (eds), *The Political Economy of Science*, London, Macmillan, 1976, p. 113.

13 Robert Ardrey, *The Territorial Imperative*, London, Collins, 1967; Desmond Morris, *The Naked Ape*, London, Cape, 1973.

14 See Martin Barker, 'Racism — the new inheritors', in *Radical Philosophy* no. 21, spring, 1979. I am grateful to Martin Barker for making me realize the importance of biologism.

15 Edward Wilson, *Sociobiology — the New Synthesis*, Harvard University Press, 1975; Richard Dawkins, *The Selfish Gene*, St Albans, Paladin, 1976.

16 Richard Dawkins, 'Sex and the immortal gene', *Vogue*, April 1977.

17 Ibid.

18 Richard Verrall, 'Sociobiology: the instinct in our genes', *Spearhead*, May 1979.

19 Steven Rose and Hilary Rose, 'The politics of neurobiology: biologism in the service of the state', in Rose and Rose (eds), op. cit., p. 107.

20 Verrall, op. cit.

21 The oppression of black people is maintained through discrimination. This becomes clear when job levels of blacks and whites are compared for different levels of education. Of those with degrees, 79 per cent of white men and 31 per cent of black men had professional or managerial jobs, while 21 per cent of blacks and no whites with degrees had manual jobs. There is clear and irrefutable evidence of consistent and massive discrimination against black people and immigrants in the fields of employment (the Civil Service, for example), housing, child benefits, health and education. See, for example, Alan Little, 'Schools and race', in *Five Views of Multi-Racial Britain*, London, Commission for Racial Equality, 1978.

22 Most of the migrants settled in cities such as Birmingham, Bradford, Manchester, London and Wolverhampton and, within these cities, in areas of cheaper housing. In London, for example, immigrants tended to concentrate in Brent, Ealing, Hackney, Haringay and North Kensington. I mention this because the statistics that are issued from these areas are not generalizable throughout the country and can be dangerously misleading.

23 What does it mean to be black? Bearing in mind that the label 'black' was invented by the whites, how is blackness perceived?

Questions such as these about ethnic identity were raised by Fanon, who was much concerned with the destruction of personality, and how the European system of education has created a colonial elite. He was antagonistic to black liberals, the poets and intellectuals who had little contact with the masses. In contrast to their stress on 'negritude', Fanon emphasized the concept of nationalism, he wanted to raise people's consciousness and liberate the oppressed by armed struggle. See David Caute, *Fanon*, London, Fontana, 1970; Frantz Fanon, *Black Skin, White Masks*, St Albans, Paladin, 1970; *The Wretched of the Earth*, Penguin, 1967.

24 Robert Jeffcoate, *Positive Image: Towards a Multiracial Curriculum*, London, Chameleon Books, 1979.

25 Bernard Coard, *How the West Indian Child is made Educationally Sub-Normal in the British School System*, London, New Beacon Books, p. 36. The most recent forms that discipline of 'recalcitrant' pupils has taken are suspensions and the setting up of Special Units for Disruptive Pupils ('sin-bins').

26 Lincoln Brown, in the *Guardian*, December 1979.

27 See, for example, David Milner, *Children and Race*, Penguin, 1975.

28 Robert Moore, *Racism and Black Resistance in Britain*, London, Pluto Press, 1975; Chris Searle, *Classrooms of Resistance*, London Writers' and Readers' Publishing Co-operative, 1975.

29 Racism is *not* a set of mistaken perceptions; this point is emphasized in Stuart Hall, *et al.*, *Policing the Crisis: Mugging, the State, Law and Order*, London, Macmillan, 1978. In Hall's view, the 'crisis' had to be explained, contained, managed, and was largely thematized through *race*; blacks became the bearers, the signifiers, of the crisis of British society. He insists that this is not a crisis *of* race. Race was the lens through which people came to perceive the crisis, it was the framework through which the crisis is experienced. There was, then, a turn towards national populism, articulated through the potent metaphors of race. Racism was no longer the preserve of a minority, it became 'naturalized', 'normal'. Racism had a popular, mobilizing appeal; there was a 'moral panic' about race which provided the basis by which a form of popular authoritarianism could be constructed.

30 '*The Visible Minority*', published by West Indian Digest, Hansib Publishing Ltd, 139-49, Fonthill Road, London N.4. Though I have stressed class analysis in this chapter, I am aware that some blacks argue that *race* has its own separate dynamic. They assert that most white workers are hostile to blacks; that trade unions and Left political parties are racist. In their view, many Marxists are mechanistic and undialectical in that they do not recognize the separate autonomous dynamic of race.

9 Summary and conclusions

1 For an analysis of how the Great Debate provided the rationale for fundamental changes in social democratic policy see James Donald, 'Green Paper: noise of crisis', *Screen Education*, no. 30, spring 1979. Donald shows that in the Labour government's Green Paper (*Education in Schools*, July 1977) the speaking subject is 'the state', and that the Great Debate was the creation and imposition of a 'new settlement' to replace the old consensus in education. He perceptively notes that there is a strengthening of central authority at the same time as an increasing public 'participation' — a move to secure consent and tighten control. Similarly, there is a strategic internationalization of capital at the same time as the promotion of localized forms of participatory democracy. In his view 'participation' is a necessary corollary of corporatism, but even participatory democracy can open up new spaces for struggle. I agree, broadly, with his conclusions that teachers should be creating an expanding layer of 'organic intellectuals'. 'Refusing and subverting the knowledge placed in power, broadcasting socialist theoretical discourses, building a counter-hegemony among cultural workers, oppositional teaching within state education, reviving radical working class education' outside the state system; these are the strategies which he suggests teachers should follow.

2 An example of such anxiety: 'Sums of money are paid by "godfathers" to terrorists to shoot a soldier or a policeman or a police officer . . . Inevitably some of the unemployed are going to get involved in this type of work. If we allow factories to close, inevitably I believe, more soldiers' lives and more policemen's lives are going to be at risk'. Lord Moyola, the former Northern Ireland Prime Minister speaking in the House of Lords; speech reported in the *Guardian*, Friday 18 July 1980.

3 It has been argued that the present moves to restructure the educational apparatus, initiated by the Great Debate cannot be understood without an effective critique of social democratic ideology on education. See Dan Finn, Neil Grant and Richard Johnson, *On Ideology*, London, Hutchinson, 1978. This article, now revised and with new conclusions, can be obtained from the Centre for Contemporary Cultural Studies, University of Birmingham, P.O. Box 363, Birmingham B15 2TT.

4 John Holloway and Sol Picciotto (eds), *State and Capital*, London, Edward Arnold, 1977.

5 Paul Bullock and David Yaffe, 'Inflation, the Crisis and the Post-War Boom', *Revolutionary Communist*, no. 3/4, November 1975.

6 Peter Leonard, 'Restructuring the Welfare State: From Social Democracy to Radical Right', *Marxism Today*, December 1979.

7 Stuart Hall, 'The great moving Right show', *Marxism Today*, January 1979; see also his article 'Thatcherism — a new stage', *Marxism Today*, February 1980.

8 Stuart Hall, *et al.*, *Policing the Crisis*, London, Macmillan, 1978.

9 CIS (Counter Information Services), *Women Under Attack*, Anti-Report no. 15, CIS, London.

10 There is a problem for socialists here. The radical Right's demand that state agencies should be cut-back and restricted, has connected with a widespread experience of bureaucratic oppression. If the state form is experienced as alien and repressive, particularly when the state is being restructured, why should the working class fight the cuts in education, health, housing, personal social services, and social security? Why should the working class defend the welfare state when the state entails alien and oppressive social relations?

11 CSE (Conference of Socialist Economists) State Group, *Cuts and Restructuring in Contemporary Britain*, London. Parents are being asked to buy essential books and equipment for schools because of the public spending cuts. However, some local authorities are reported to be spending more money on buying places in independent schools than on books for their own schools (*Guardian*, Monday 30 June 1980). The numbers at private schools have increased despite the fact that fees are increasing faster than inflation.

12 But he remarks: 'I ask the pardon of those teachers who, in dreadful conditions, attempt to turn the few weapons they can find in the history and learning they 'teach' against the ideology, the system and the practices in which they are trapped. They are a kind of hero.' Louis Althusser, 'Ideology and ideological state apparatuses', in *Lenin and Philosophy and Other Essays*, London, New Left Books, 1971; also in B.R. Cosin (ed.), *Education: Structure and Society*, Penguin, 1972, p. 261.

13 CSE, *Struggle Against the State*; CSE, *In and Against the State*, obtainable from CSE Books, 55, Mount Pleasant, London WC1X 0AE.

14 See, for example, Stephen Castles and Wiebke Wustenberg, *The Education of the Future*, London, Pluto Press, 1979; Theodore Norton and Bertell Ollman (eds), *Studies in Socialist Pedagogy*, New York, Monthly Review Press, 1978.

Index